Franchise Of The Year!

by
Peter Crouch

Franchise Of The Year!

Content advisory. This book contains references that may be considered suitable for adults only: sexual references, adult language.

Published in the USA.

Published by Chargan My Book Publisher Pty. Ltd.
Level 18
152 St Georges Tce
Perth, WA, Australia 6000

www.chargan.com

ISBN 978-1-4478-1444-3

Dedication

I would like to dedicate the book to my lovely wife Marinka, and all my customers over the last five years, without them, this book would have been impossible to write.

I tell Marinka how lucky she is too having me. She tells me how lucky I am that she puts up with me everyday! No one else would.

This book is also dedicated to all those people that are thinking of buying a franchise.

Foreword

To anyone thinking of buying a franchise:

The key word is "beware". Franchisors are out to make money, please read the small print, as it's too late once you have signed the contract.

There are many Franchisors that are not greedy or self opinionated.

The best franchisors would be run by a board of Directors that are accountable for their actions, with a breakdown on all spending. Remember you are paying for their company, without franchisees, there would be no Franchise.

If any of you are thinking that they are buying a job, or going to semi-retire, think again, your hard-earned money over the years won't last long, when you still have to pay fees every week, even when you are not turning over enough money.

What happens when you are ill, take holidays, have a family crisis? They still require their fees.

I love my job, more so for the people I have met along the way.

Would I do it again? Good question.

The answer would have to be yes, but as my own business.

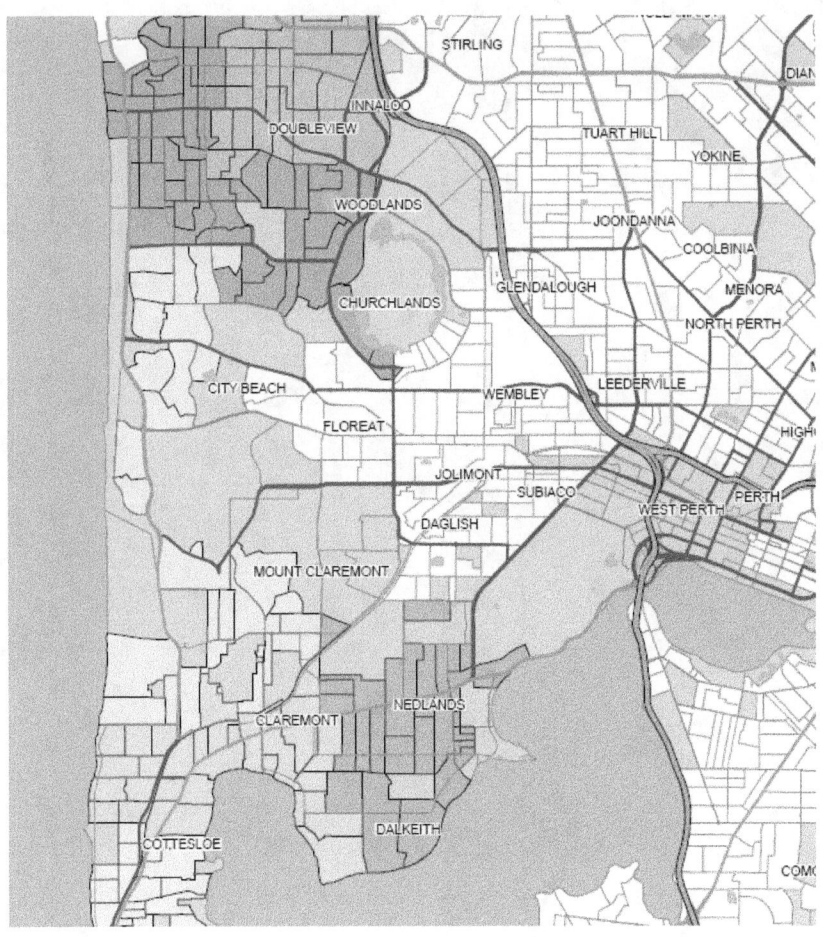

Perth suburbs referred to in this book.
Note: some suburb names and client names have been
changed to respect the privacy of clients.

Contents

Surprise all round

One of the funniest and completely innocent experiences was when a lady booked in a job to clean her carpets on a Monday, but didn't want me to start till 12.30 pm as she was a paramedic and had been working all weekend on the graveyard shift.

She told me she wanted to get the house clean for when her partner returned, as he had been working away for 3 weeks and she couldn't wait until he got home later that afternoon.

Hence she wanted a lie in so that she wasn't tired when he got home.

I got around there about 12.30. While I was cleaning the carpets, she was busy cleaning the rest of the house, getting it ready so they could relax that evening when he returned.

I brought in my Eftpos machine as usual, as most pay by card nowadays, and wrote out the invoice. She paid by cash, had a quick chat and said goodbye.

I drove to my 2 o'clock job and started to unload my van when I realised that I had left my Eftpos machine at the last house on her table. I rang her up and asked if that was the case. She said yes, so I told her I would call around later on the way home from work to pick it up. All good.

I finished my last job about 4.30 pm and drove back to her house. As I pulled in to her drive a car pulled up alongside me. I didn't take much notice, got out and walked around the side gate, been there before so didn't bother to knock.

The guy who was in the car was walking a few yards behind me. I still didn't take much notice. As I was walking up the drive, her dog starting barking, letting her know that someone was there.

I was just about to knock on the door, when it flew open with the lady wearing just a pair of knickers!

1

She was shouting out 'surprise', in a spread eagle position, when with one look at me she screamed and ran in behind the door!

I turned around to look at the guy behind me and said "I've only come back for my Eftpos machine honestly"!

He just grinned and said "I think she got more of a surprise then you! I just texted her to say I will be home in 5 minutes."

"Oh shit" I said "she thought I was you!"

"That would be it. I'd better get your machine for you." So he popped in and returned still smiling. "Thanks" I said and left, probably for the last time.

How we started

That was just one of many funny but true stories, that I would come home and tell my wife Marinka and daughter Carly.

They both, along with some of my friends, would say I should write a book about the running of a carpet cleaning franchise.

My answer would always be: "who would believe me?"

This is how it all began.

I bought the franchise five years ago. I'm a Plumber by trade or more to the point a sheet roofing plumber, or even more to the point a sheet lead worker.

I came to Oz to be with my now wife Marinka to start a new life, and being a plumber here was the last thing I wanted to do for a number of reasons, most of them best left unsaid.

I was in the middle of a real estate course, when an old friend of mine (now ex-friend) also from England had just acquired a franchise of a carpet cleaning business. He asked me if I would be interested in joining him as a partner in buying another two franchises, making three in total.

My answer to him was, "who the fuck has their carpets cleaned?"

His reply was "you would be surprised."

So I worked for him for two weeks to try it out. We fell out, as you guessed, over money, so what happened was that I parted company with him and obtained my own franchise of carpet cleaning.

As you know, we own a franchise of a well known carpet cleaning company. There over 140 franchises throughout Australia. They are one of the biggest if not the largest carpet cleaners in Australia. There are bigger ones elsewhere in the world, though that is not very important to our story.

Franchise Of The Year!

In 2010 we became Franchise Of The Year!

However the franchisor had not wanted to give me the title. We don't always see eye to eye. That would be the best description of our relationship. I think he's a greedy, self centered dictator, who tries to treat us all like employees, and believes we are incapable of thinking for ourselves.

But we are ok in working our own franchises and paying high fees, plus 10% of any income above the base turnover of $3500 per week, plus we pay over $800 a week on advertising, so really they do very little for our fees. We don't even get a say in where our advertising money goes. We might, but it falls on deaf ears.

The advantage for buying a franchise is that the base is already in place.

They have structure and a marketing plan, which may be not a good one, plus a guaranteed customer base, with exciting customers, a proven formula, and you would think, a backup and help service for the franchisees. Not all true.

How do you get started?

You have to buy the area from the previous owner. He gives the franchisor 10% of the sale, why I don't know, but we will have to when we sell. They encourage you to build up your area at your cost, so you can pay them an extra 10% of all income per month, and hopefully you haven't gone bankrupt beforehand when you sell!

The idea is to have two or more vans in one area, as your franchise fees and advertising are the same, but your over and above income is obviously charged at 10%.

The problem is getting good technicians for the van.

Buying another van, and set of equipment, etc even a second hand van of any use, would set you back at least $20,000. To fully equip it with an extraction machine, polisher, vacuum, bonnet pads, spray bottles, rakes, horse hair brushes (for lounge suites), chemicals etc, would cost at least $6000 second hand, and at least $15,000 new.

So to put the van on the road, the minimum it would cost you would be $26,000. Then on top of that you have to pay wages, mobile phone, fuel, maintenance cost, repair or renewal costs, plus loss of income, while they are being repaired.

That is without the worry of getting enough work every day of the year. I say everyday because they charge franchise fees and advertising for 52 weeks. No holidays, you might be thinking, not if you buy one of these franchises.

If the company was owned by us, I am sure I wouldn't be invoicing Christmas week, or the two weeks I take for a holiday.

When we first started, all franchises took their own calls and bookings. Head office would take the odd franchisees calls if they couldn't cope or when franchisees when on holiday, for a couple of weeks. They also used to redirect the odd stray call.

About eighteen months ago, in their infinite wisdom, they decided to start up a call centre in the Philippines, using they say American university educated girls, paying them peanuts I don't doubt.

They wanted everyone to join this call centre, making it sound so good, but only a handful of franchisees, probably the ones head office in Newcastle NSW were doing anyway, took up their offer.

We suspected that it was started as a control move. They would have access to everybody's booking system and know how many jobs were booked in and for how much, controlling not only your day but your complete business.

They said your job to phone call ratio would increase by 20%.

As nobody took the up on their kind offer, they then said, not that it was in any of our contracts, that anybody owing them more than $15,000 for more than 60 days or anyone with less that 40% conversion rate i.e. jobs to calls, would have to go on to the call centre, at just under $200 per week, this is on top of our advertising, franchise fees, 13---- phone number fees, chemicals, and day to day running costs.

Great earner for them: low set up costs, low rent and cheap labour in the Philippines, some tables and desks, a few computers. Not much more than that. I am sure they think we are all stupid or too small indivisibly, to stand up to them.

Just think if 100 out of the 145 franchises were to pay them for their kind service then that's $20,000 per week times 52, because we would still have to pay Christmas week and when we are sick, or on holiday, then they earn $1,040,000 per year from the poxy business.

If we were all to use it like they wanted us to, it would be $1,508,000.

That is over a million dollars profit each year in somebody's pocket. Not ours.

Also it would look good if they wanted to sell the Franchise, total control, with a side show bringing in over a million dollars profit.

He might be a greedy dictator, but he is not stupid.

We had to use the call centre for a few months as we got in to debt with them for a while, when Marinka was ill.

Our conversion rate went done from 70% to 50%. Our customers said they would stop using us, if they had to call the call centre, saying that they had to wait up to 5 minutes to talk to someone, then sometimes would be left on hold, which could only be due to short staff or lack of phones.

Once answered, the customers found them hard to understand, with a Philippine American ascent. They all said that they were friendly, to the point of sickly, kept asking them to repeat their details, could not pronounce their names or suburbs correctly, and tried to up-sell on the phone all the time.

Also they could not answer some questions when asked. Sometimes my regular customers would be on the phone for up to twenty minutes just to book in three rooms, which should take at tops five minutes.

Everybody took my personal mobile number so they could call me direct which ruined the whole idea of the call centre, and could cause a black market trade.

They just never thought the whole thing through properly. If you're in Australia you want to speak to an Australian. It doesn't matter how many of us, which is most of us, tell them, they don't want to change it.

They had no choice but to give me Franchise Of The Year. Our turnover and conversion rate of jobs to phone calls received were over 80% whereas their average is only 40%, including their call centre in Asia, which I disagree with and won't use for a number of reasons, best left unsaid in the book.

I never really wanted to be Franchise Of The Year, and it's not that I am cleverer than any other franchisee. I just happen to have a very affluent franchise zone with some of the richest areas in Perth. Also the Franchisor told me two years ago that it would be impossible to have 3 vans running in one area. I went out to prove him wrong, and he had to back down which I know would have killed him. During the conference when I was awarded the Franchise Of The Year, my nickname was Foy.

Over the last 5 years we have also added commercial work, like real-estate agents, hotels, and small businesses, which I would say are our bread and butter. The work that is generated by our Franchisors head office only provides work in the private sector, and for most of us not enough to keep a substantial franchise in full swing.

In one particular hotel, we do quite a lot of call out work for drink spills on carpets and upholstery, sometimes, ink, crayon, alcohol, and baby formula. Also we have had to clean four mattresses due to bed wetting.

During the March storms they had two rooms and the conference room flooded. We are probably there on average once a week.

What I didn't realise was that when you book into a hotel and they ask you for credit card details, they will charge you with any damage if anything needs professional cleaning. I always thought that they took your credit card details, just in case you used the bar fridge or ate in their restaurant.

While I was cleaning one of the floors the head, a clean nice middle aged woman, came to ask me to look at a lounge suite with ink on in another room. "Some of the people are like pigs" I said, "I am sure they wouldn't do this in their own house." "You would hope not" she said. "I bet you see some sights."

I said, "I have been doing this for years and nothing surprises me now."

The worst are the middle aged men. When the young girls come to clean their rooms and knock on the doors, a lot of the time they don't answer, so the girls knock again and enter. Just when they walk in the men walk out naked, saying "oh sorry I didn't hear you, I was having a shower." It happens too often to be a mistake, at least three to four times a week.

I wonder if they just get their kicks from it, or are hoping the girls will come on to them? A bit of both I would imagine.

We have had this franchise for 5 years, mostly good, but hard work. When we started both Marinka and I used to work it, Marinka taking the phone calls and bookings, and doing the book work, myself on the road, doing the cleaning, and at week-ends both on the van together.

It took a long time to build up to the clientele. Now we have just over 5,000 customers.

When we first took over we were only turning over $1,500 to $2,000 per week, which was less than our outgoings, as our fees to the franchisor are more than $1,500 per week, plus 10% for any work more than $3,500 per week, plus chemicals, fuel, phones, computers, stationary, insurances, accountant, the list goes on.

We give quotes over the phone, depending what the caller tells us (not all tell the truth), and then adjust the price when on site. That is where the trouble begins. This is where we find out what percentage they are, good, ok, or arsehole.

After 2 years, we were doing quite well, and decided to buy another franchise, which came up quite cheap or so it seemed at the time, south of the river. We would have a technician work it for us. We soon discovered why it was so cheap, the last franchisee had run it right down, and it had a bad reputation. We went through several technicians, most useless or greedy or lazy. I found I was trying to work both franchisees, which was killing me, paying double franchisee fees, for little or no return each month.

Marinka then became very ill with cancer of the Douglas pouch, which we found out is inside a women's bits, so named after the man that found it. Strange, I've been looking all my life and never found it. Marinka had to have radiotherapy for about a year, and became extremely ill at times, with her immune system very low. I also found things extremely hard to cope with, and got quite depressed at times, which would sometimes last for months.

That was probably our lowest point. We got into financial problems of course and couldn't see a way out at one point.

Then Marinka got the all clear.

We decided to sell the second franchise, build up the other one to two vans, while only paying one lot of franchisee fees. Marinka went back to what she knew best - Pharmacy.

I took over the phone calls and bookings, tried to get other people doing the bookinsg for me but that didn't work out, found I was best at it myself, and it was a lot easier to control. We got a second van on the road and employed Jason who was great, well most of the time, and he could sell on.

We had a second wage coming in, which was great, and worked our way out of our problems, well almost.

It will take a long time to get back to where we were, probably a few more years, but we have both been strong together, and found it had made us closer if that's possible. Most couples would probably not have survived it.

Two years on we won Franchise Of The Year. We are both quite proud of that achievement.

They try to hold a conference every eighteen months, using a different venue each time. Our first one was in the Hunter Valley. It rained every day of the three days we were there. We all got lost on the way and didn't arrive till three in the morning. The first meeting was at 8.30 am, not well organised at all. Our chalets were at the bottom of the hill and the conference at the top. The roads turned into a mud bath, we were thinking this company couldn't organise a piss up in a brewery, but we all made the best of it.

The second conference was a top hotel in Brisbane, much better, good hotel, great rooms, swimming pool, no rain. It was at that conference that we met the new managing director. We got on extremely well. He came across as straight, honest, friendly, and with a sense of humour. We found we had a lot in common. He is an Italian Indian, educated in London England, and followed the English soccer premiership. Over the next 18 months we kept in touch, and he helped us a lot when we were having our problems.

At the next conference which was on the Sunshine Coast, another good venue, Marinka and I went out drinking a couple of times. At gala/ presentation night, the last night, we had all been drinking. There was a group of us franchisees all together, with the managing director.

Now you need to understand that at conferences, everybody moans to everybody, and a lot of the franchisees thought he was an arrogant prick, and not very helpful. I always stuck up for him because that was not how I found him.

Well back to Gala Night. We were all standing there, after the presentations. We came 3rd, I might add, believing that's as far as we would ever get. We were all drinking in the smokers room, probably about thirty of us.

Then I turned around to the M.D. and said "most of us believe you are an arrogant arse, but I will say it to your face, and not behind your back". He just stared at me and smiled and said "fuck off you're more arrogant than me". We then started arguing about who was the most arrogant, when we stopped and looked around.

All the other Franchisees were gone, and the only person left was Marinka with her head in her hands not believing what I had said.

"Sorry" she said to the M.D., "Peter says what he thinks, but at least he tells you to your face." "Don't worry" he said "let's get another drink, and drink to honest, straight forward talking people." With that we shook on it and agreed.

If it was not for him, eighteen months later I would not have won Franchise Of The Year.

Not that we just clean carpets, oh no more than that my friends, we also clean upholstery, drapes, leather, and tile and grout, listen to old ladies telling us about their departed husbands, their children, look at old photos of their past, and we also play with kids, look at their drawings from school, see their new toys, pat dogs, move furniture, pick up clothes including underwear and a whole lot more as you will find out while reading this story of the life of a carpet cleaner!

All the franchisees attend special training, and update courses to make sure we are abreast of anything new in the industry, but the job is as only as good as the technician doing the job, and like any job there are some crap ones out there. Not many but a few I know, that I would not recommend.

I've have a few jobs, owned my own Plumbing and Roofing company, taught for two years at a technical college, had a fish and chip shop and owned a pub/ restaurant for two years. I thought the pub was an eye opener to the general public, I could tell some stories there, but another time. I've always said after the pub, that I had seen and heard it all and that nothing could shock me anymore, and maybe that's true, but I am still surprised by people every day.

Quite often, while we are cleaning people's houses, they ask us about tile and grout clean. What I always do is say would you like me to clean a small section, so you can see how will it will come up, but you must understand that this is done by hand the big clean comes up so much better as it's done with machines.

I then give them a brochure, and ask them which tile to test. They always say in the kitchen, and I always say that tile there, pointing to the middle tile, looks the worst. Ok they say.

I then clean the middle tile by hand, using an alkaline chemical, tile and grout brush, and clean damp, cotton nappy.

When I am finished, they can't believe the difference, and go "well I will have to get it done now". Their husbands if there will say "you wanker, you deliberately did the middle tile, so we have to clean the rest." "I asked what tile" I always say, but you're right, I did.

Good on you, you say, a good way to generate work. Nine times out of ten they book the job in straightaway.

I've had a few accidents at work, also a couple in the van. Due to the vans being quite wide, with quite a few drives being narrow and overgrown, we quite often clip overgrown trees, when reversing out, and on one occasion, I turned too sharply and caught a carport post, which slowly bent lowering its roof until I realised what I had done.

I then had to go forward and reverse past it and then drive into it to straighten it up, did quite a good job, never quite looked the same, but never had a complaint though. Got away with that one!

When I first started our shirts, which were light blue with dark blue collar and cuffs, use to be the same as the local high school, in one of our suburbs we work in.

One day Jason and myself were standing in the queue at MacDonald's one lunch time. Now you must realise we are both six foot, and weight about 100 kilos, when about thirty school boys walked in, we both felt like we where the big kids of the class. The girl behind the counter asked us if our mum knew if we were having MacDonald's for lunch!

Two years ago we decided to purchase a new van. Our second van was past its sell by date, and to expand we realised it was best to purchase a new van, because the government was giving a 50% tax rebate benefit on any new commercial purchases if bought before the end of the tax year. The first port of call was head office. We imagined that they would know where the best place to purchase one was, where to get the sign writing done, and hopefully the cheapest way to finance it.

They were very helpful. He put us in contact with Marc who had done several deals with other franchises in the eastern states, and they had found him extremely helpful, efficient, and the quickest and cheapest deal. We also found him extremely friendly helpful, intelligent, and efficient, especially for a 28 year old man. He had an old head on young shoulders. I also like to deal with people I like and trust, and Marc comes high up that list for both.

Also he coordinated between garage, sign writers, and interior fit-out. The van was purchased from a Sydney dealer, where they sent the sign writers, where the interior was made to fit our equipment, and storage shelves for the chemicals.

Even if we had bought the van in Perth, it would still have had to be transported to Sydney, for the signage on the van, and then to be given the ok after inspection by them that it was completely correct.

It took about 4 months going backwards and forward with e-mails, mainly due to the sign work and interior fit out, we were stuck in a queue until finally we had a delivery date, but that was not good, they wanted $2,000 and stated it would take 17 days. I asked if they were delivering in on the Orient Express.

So after discussing it, Marinka and I decided that we would fly to Sydney, pick up the van, and drive it back. We had always fancied the

13

trip, and it should save us about $1,000, two weeks on the delivery date, and have some fun on the way.

So that is what we did. I ordered new personalized plates for the van 'RUGMEN'. We arranged to drive the van back with no plates on. We arrived in Sydney on Thursday morning, had arranged to meet Marc at 7 o'clock that evening, at a Chinese restaurant for dinner. It would be the first time we would have met, with all our dealings have been on the phone. I knew he was a Manchester United supporter, so we brought him a Spurs beanie.

We all still have the drunken photos of us all with him wearing the beanie. I believe he has the photo on his wall, to remind him of that unusual night.

We decided to do a bit of sightseeing, while we were there, and took the ferry over the harbour, had lunch and then had a bit of a look around, got the ferry back quite early, to allow us to get showered and changed ready to meet Marc at 7 pm.

Unfortunately we got off at the wrong stop and got lost, and it took us over an hour to get back to the hotel. Marinka now really annoyed as we had been travelling all day, and she had not had time to wash her hair. We had quick showers, got changed, and walked down to meet Marc.

We met him outside, said our hi's and went into the restaurant, got our table and opened the wine Marc had brought with him.

While we were waiting for our meal, we had drunk the wine, so I got up and got both Marc and myself a pint of Stella and a Jack Daniels and coke each. We all chatted away during dinner, telling stories about ourselves, decided that we wouldn't be that late tonight as we had arranged to pick the van up at 9 am so we could leave quite early, so we could make our way back to Perth. We wanted to be back by Sunday night, ready for work Monday.

We all got on like a house on fire. During our meal we bought some more drinks, now we were at the point that we needed a couple more drinks, but decided to leave the restaurant and find a pub along the harbour. Found a couple of pubs and then ended up on a pub crawl along the harbour, until Marc decided to get a cab into Kings Cross. We ended in a strip joint until 4 am, all slightly pissed. We got a cab back home, and the driver dropped us off at the hotel, after dropping Marc home.

I was up 7 am in the morning, made a cup of tea and tried to wake Marinka up. No chance! She was suffering from a hangover, so I went out for a walk and had a cigarette.

When I got back I woke Marinka, got ready to wait for Marc to pick us up at 8.30 am to take us to collect the van. 8.30 came and went, 9 am came and I decided to call him. Hello he said on the phone, still asleep and not sounding very well. He had overslept, and had a wicked hangover, and said he would be 45 minutes. I am lucky as I don't suffer from hangovers ever since I owned a pub in Norfolk in England, a few years ago.

Marc turns up at 10.30, as white as a sheet! We left in Marc's car, found a good cafe, and while Marinka slept in the back of the car, Marc and I ate a good full English breakfast, and then felt a lot better. When we got back to the car Marinka was still fast asleep, so we drove to the dealership to finally pick up our new van, for our drive back to Perth.

We had a great time driving back, both sharing the driving. Mind you I got lost leaving Sydney as Marinka fell asleep again. We stopped at some interesting places, and meet some interesting and odd people on the way back.

I asked Marc for his email address, he told me it was

cuppymayland @ ------.

"Why cuppymayland?" I asked.

"Well he said, it's a bit embarrassing but when I was 16 years old I was an apprentice car mechanic and on my 17th birthday, my mum came in to the garage at lunch time and brought in some cup cakes for everyone. After that my nickname was cup cake, than as I got older to Cuppy. Lots of my old friends know me by that name.

Marc and myself have kept in contact with each other ever since, and both still tell people about that night we all first met in Sydney. His boss still gives him stick over that one.

Only the other day, while speaking to Marc on the phone, he told me a great story, about his holiday in Phuket, Thailand, last Christmas.

He and his wife were going diving with a large English group, diving from a boat a couple of miles offshore. While on the charter boat for the first time, Marc being Marc, to break the ice asked out loud who supports what football club. His replies were Spurs, Chelsea, Aston Villa etc, they said to him I bet you are a Manchester United fan being an Australian, glory hunter, he told them that he had supported Man U since he was a kid.

Well there was an elderly lady who was 84 years old, she and her husband had supported Tottenham Hotspurs all her life, she lost her husband about two years ago, and was now doing something she had always wanted to do - scuba driving. Marc said she was great, only did one dive a day and not four like the rest of them, but was really good and was always one of the last ones back up.

Joking she said to Marc while they were all out drinking one night, she was going to get the Cockerel of Spurs tattooed on her bum, they laughed thinking of an 84 year old having a tattoo on her arse.

By the end of the week they had all gone their own ways, Marc and his wife arrived at the airport to fly back to Australia, when they arrived at the airport they saw a coach carrying the English group. As they waved to them, the elderly lady run down to the back of the coach, dropped her pants, mooned him, and tattooed on her arse was the cockerel of Spurs!

I am on the road every day doing between three and five jobs and moving from suburb to suburb. Because I answer my own phones for work, I have ear phones in the work phone, but also get work calls previous customers, recommendations, and real estate agents, on my personal phone.

I must admit, when I am in traffic, I do answer that phone sometimes, which has got me in trouble with the police on more than one occasion. Some have booked me, but a few have let me off with a warning, with me promising I won't do it again. I can't anymore as now I am on a special good behaviour licence for 12 months. Not all my points are for the phone: some are for speeding, and one was for speeding one public holiday, double demerit points.

I had a lucky escape one day. I was travelling down Stirling Highway, in heavy traffic, having just left one job and on the way to my next job. I had my seat belt on, but when the phone rang I undid it to get my phone out of my pocket, and without thinking, I answered it. If you miss a call, a lot of the time people will just call the next carpet cleaner, and works work.

Anyway alongside was a police van that told me to move over. Obviously I didn't see him when I answered the phone. We pulled over and he told me off, which I deserved, and took my licence that had run out the day before, not going good I thought. "You're not the Peter Crouch that plays for Spurs" he asked. "No I wouldn't be cleaning carpets if I was." "Suppose not" he said.

"Look I understand you need to run a business, and you have ear phones in for one phone, but there's no excuse for not wearing a seat belt." "No you are right", I said, "but I undid it to get my phone out of my pocket." He just shook his head. "I just came out from Dalkeith Road, and forgot to put it back on, I am sorry."

"Where are you going to?" he asked. "Just down the road to Claremont."

"Ok" he said, "I have to book you for something, so I am just going to do you for no seat belt, but I won't put it through until tomorrow, which will give you time to go on the Internet and sort out your licence, and go online and get a dual sim card for your phone so you only need one set of ear phones."

17

"Thanks "I said "that's very kind of you."

"That's ok I have a brother who's a plumber, he has the same problem as you." "Thanks anyway you still didn't have to do that." "I did it because you accepted you were in the wrong, didn't argue, and was genuinely sorry." "Thanks again" I said.

About one month later I was in a BP garage in Karrinyup, waiting for my morning coffee, when two coppers walked in, and ordered their coffee.

Just standing there checking my emails on the phone, one of the coppers said "hi Peter how are you."

I looked at him, not sure how he knew my name when he said, "you don't remember me do you, I pulled you over about a month ago, on Stirling Highway. I remember your name because of the footballer."

"I remember" I said, "and thanks again for that, I've just ordered the dual sim for my phone." "Good" he said, "have a good day." "You too."

I have been going to the same bank now for the last five years, at least two to three times a week. You get to know the staff quite well, when you go in that many times, and with most of them, as they change quite frequently, I have been on first name terms. It helps in long queues, especially on a Friday afternoon, for some reason. Quite often if they see me queuing they call me to the front, which embarrasses both Marinka and Carly as they can see the faces of the people in front of us. I just don't look, too grateful not to queue as it's a pet hate of mine.

Quite often now if I know the girl on the front desk, I go straight there.

How Carpet and Upholstery cleaning works

The basic carpet cleaning is as follows:

- the carpets are pre-vacuumed,
- then an alkaline pre-spray is sprayed on the carpet, left for a few minutes,
- then a bonnet pad is dipped in an acidic rinse and put onto the carpet,
- a rotary polisher is then placed on top of the bonnet pad, and turned on.

The idea is that the alkaline breaks down the oils and greases, and releases the dirt, then the acidic rinse neutralises the carpet and helps to remove any stains that are acidic. The pads are changed frequently for new clean ones. After the carpets have been cleaned, they are raked to bring up the pile, and to help dry the carpets, which normally takes about 45 minutes to an hour and half, depending on the weather. We also steam clean if the carpets are really bad, or there is vomit, blood or urine, but at an extra cost.

Upholstery and stairs are cleaned with an extraction machine after they have been vacuumed, pre-sprayed and brushed. Then an upholstery tool is moved slowly over the area to be cleaned. The upholstery tool sprays water with a rinse aid in, to both neutralise the alkaline pre-spray cleaner, and condition the fabric. Drapes are done in similar fashion.

Tile and grout has to be cleaned with an alkaline or non-acidic solution, alkaline only for natural stone or slate, otherwise it would etch the tiles with the acid.

Then we use a high powered tool with a large turbo head. It has internal jets spraying at up to a thousand psi and internal vacuum, removing the dirty water and pumping it to waste.

That's only the beginning of running the business. The first port of call is answering the phone in a correct manner.

First impressions go a long way, and answering in a professional but friendly manner will help to put the potential customer at ease.

Being able to answer all their questions straight away is important: giving them a good idea of costs and variations, different ways of cleaning, firm booking time, what furniture and small personal items they should move, and how long the job should take, and lastly, payment methods.

Next, not only should the technician be in a uniform, but be clean and tidy, and clean shaven, and not smelling like a dust bin even on the hottest day! Being on time, if running more than 15 minutes late, we call just to let them know. There's nothing worse than waiting for a tradesperson to arrive. There is no excuse nowadays with mobile phones.

Overall it is important to do a good a job, remembering that you are in somebody's house with all their personal belongings, so they must trust you without a doubt.

Everyone works differently, but the basics must be the same.

After a hard day's work, it's back home to book all the jobs in the computer, do any invoicing and bookwork and cleaning the dirty bonnets for the next day, and cleaning out the van. That should leave a couple of hours to shower, eat, dinner, and spend some time with the family.

In the first couple of weeks while I was working, and learning, with the other franchisee, (ex-friend), we went to a large two story house in Trigg. When we got there we were met by a black English guy from Birmingham who had been renting the property for the last twelve months, and he was moving out, as his lease had run out.

"It needs some work" he said, "we had a party at the weekend, and there's some paint in the kids bedroom. I will show you around and leave you to it. I have to go back to work."

Well you should have seen the place!

It was a stunning house, but wrecked. The front lounge had beer, wine, soft drinks and cigarette ash trodden into it.

It was white carpet, turned black. The study wasn't much better, and when we went into the three bedrooms at the rear, both boys rooms carpets were completely painted, except where the beds would have been before the rooms were emptied. One was painted blue, the colour of Birmingham City Football club, the other claret for Aston Villa Football club. The girl's room was covered in makeup.

Not that it mattered to us but the kitchen was filthy, with grease all over the floor, along with food and drink spills, shit all over the work tops and the stairs leading to the master bedroom and family retreat, which should have been white, were black. Even the adult retreat and bedroom had drink and cigarette ash all over it.

We said "you must be kidding, the place is a wreck. Why did you let the kids paint the carpets? You will never get these carpets back to normal, or even close. You are better off losing your bond and paying towards new carpets."

He said "I know we won't get our bond back, but I just want to try and clean them as it's in our contract."

"We have never seen anything this bad" we said. "It's not only my kids", he said "my wife's sister and husband and their kids also lived here."

"She was babysitting while we were all at work and had some friends over, and we left the kids in their rooms. When she went to find them because they had been quiet for so long, she found they had painted their carpets with water colour from their painting sets, for a laugh."

"I bet you're not laughing now."

"The only way we have any chance of bringing the carpets to any kind of a reasonable standard is if we do a dual clean, on all the rooms, plus sanitise each room" I said.

21

Franchise Of The Year!

"How much will that cost" he asked.

"$240 for the 7 rooms, $60 for the stairs, plus $200 for the extraction cleaner, to suck up all the paint, alcohol and food etc, then $11 per room to sanitise, that's $577."

"Christ" he said. "I will have to ask my brother in law."

He made the phone call, agreed and went back to work, leaving us to carry on.

We did exactly what we said. The paint in the boy's bedrooms, and the make up in the girls, as it was all water based, came out with the extraction clean, but the rest of the carpets still looked grey in colour. After the bonnet clean the bedrooms and stairs looked great, but the lounge, study, and adult retreat, only looked ok. We then sanitised the carpets, to kill any germs and to make them smell nice. Green apple smell.

When he came back he was quite pleasantly shocked!

One day we were so busy that Marinka had to collect some chemicals for me in our first old van as I just didn't have the time.

She picked them up from one of our suppliers in Osborne Industrial Park, and she left the suppliers in a rush, after they had helped her load up. This was in the early years when Marinka was sorting out the phone calls and bookings.

As she drove quickly out of a side road, onto Scarborough Beach Road, which is a main road, the back of the van sprang open, dispersing all the new chemicals, spray bottles, racks, buckets etc, all over the road!

The traffic came to a stand still for 30 minutes, while crying of embarrassment, and anger, she and a couple of other drivers helped throw all the bits as quickly as they could back into the van, while the phone was ringing at the same time.

She then had to pull over and pick up all the messages, before driving to me, to deliver all of the chemicals.

By the time she got to me she had calmed down, but could not see the funny side for a few days.

"How about me?" I said, "I had to sort all the van out, after you threw my stuff all over Scarborough Beach Road, and didn't put it back properly."

No wonder she didn't see the funny side of it at the time. I still smile today watching her face as I had a light-hearted go at her. I have to admit it had happened to me a few times in the old van, when the rear door catch didn't always close properly. It used to slowly rise up, twice going down the Freeway it came open, but I never lost a thing.

Customers and People

This job is an insight to everyone's walk of life from rich to poor, clever to dim, clean to downright dirty. We go inside everyone's home and into all their private rooms. This is where life begins and my stories start, most of them funny, some sad, most unbelievable, but all true.

'There's nowt as queer as folk' they say. Let me tell you, that is an understatement.

90% of people are nice, 5% are ok and 5% are complete arseholes.

You meet them all doing this job, you also get to learn how different nationalities think, i.e. Indians and most Asians have to barter so you have to put on 10% to give them 10% discount so they feel that they have a bargain and you get the correct price for the job.

Most people from the UK have to know how long you have been doing the job, and doubt your ability and think they are going to be ripped off.

Oz women are great and down to earth and Oz men, well, they are what the rest of the world think they are. Not all, but most.

Greeks and Italians ask you thousands of questions but if they like and trust you they tell all their friends and family how good you are. If they don't then you're shit and everyone will know.

South Africans come across arrogant, but I believe that it is just their accent, because one of my favourite customers is South African, more about her later, now that is a funny story.

I have only walked away from one job, and that was about 2 years ago. Now you have to remember there are snobs in this world, and carpet cleaning is carpet cleaning and you don't have to be the brightest, but what they will never understand is that we are actually running a business and have to learn about the manufacturing of all carpets, upholstery, tiles, how pH values effect different materials and liquids, etc. otherwise we could cause quite a bit of damage to peoples possessions.

Now that job I walked away from, this lady booked her job in, stating it was for 4 rooms for the price of $119, of which we had a special on at the time.

On arriving the first thing she said to me as I pulled up on her drive was, "I hope your van doesn't leak oil."

As I had just had it cleaned, bearing in mind my van was less than 6 months old, I just gave her that look of 'I can't be bothered to even reply to that one'.

The next statement was "you are 10 minutes late. I've been waiting all morning. You could have called to say you were going to be late."

Our policy is to call people if we are going to be more than 15 minutes late and they are told that when making a booking, but these people don't hear that, only what they want to hear. I have learned that these people try to make you feel lower class straight away, I believe that they do it so they can dictate to you what you are doing and for how much, because 'I'm cleverer than you and you should know your place'.

I just smile and say "you obviously didn't understand me when you were told on the phone that we call if we are going to be more than 15 minutes late. If you couldn't understand me I could have repeated it for you."

So in I went. 4 rooms my arse, she had 7 rooms, 4 bed rooms and a lounge/dining the size of an aircraft hanger, maybe slightly over the top, but any way it was big.

Now our rooms are based on 13 m^2 and everybody is told this, when booking it is also in our brochures and advertising sheets.

So I said this is not 4 rooms but 7 so the price for 7 rooms is $207 that's still getting one room free. Well she insisted that the one large aircraft hanger was only one room, and her last carpet cleaner only charged her for 4 rooms.

"Get him back then" I said packing away my equipment.

"You can't leave", she said, I've just moved everything ready for you.

"Just watch me, if you don't want to pay the correct price for the job than that's not my problem."

"Ok" she said "but you have to clean my 3 rugs as well."

No answer from me as I walked out the door with my equipment.

"Where are you going" she asked.

"To my next customer who pays the correct price for the job without the bullshit" I replied.

"I am going to call your boss" she said as she called our company number, and got me saying "hello, thank you for calling ----------- this is Peter speaking how can I help you?"

"It's you" she said still speaking on the phone but looking at me.

"Yes I own it" I said, and walked away.

"You will never work for me or any of my friends and family" she said.

"Well thanks for that because if they are anything like you I don't want to" and left!

You have to laugh at these *nouveau riche* people!

My wife and I went to a house in Nedlands to clean the carpets, quite a nice trendy house in a good suburb. Still waiting after 20 minutes I finally called him, and 5 minutes later he arrives in his nice BMW 320i with an apology for being late. He then shows us what he wants done in an arrogant manner as if we were stuck to his shoe and walked off, leaving us to move all his tables and chairs etc. without any help from him.

I had no time for him, but Marinka saw he had a photo of him skiing on the wall. As we had just come back from Queenstown NZ skiing she asked him where the ski resort was. He in his 'what would you know' manner said Thredbo NSW.

"Why, do you ski?" he asked.

"Yes," she said "but we prefer Europe or Canada, more up market and better facilities and runs, more for the advanced skiers though."

"Oh" he said, and his attitude completely changed. Snob. When we were about to leave we went to the bathroom to wash our hands and in the bath his cat had shit in the bath, karma I think.

I sometimes wonder about this small percentage of snobby middle class people who think they are above the lower classes (in their mind) they believe they have done well in life because they are clever and work harder than the working class and poor. They can see that many people are where they are in life because life dictates our destiny sometimes without our control, be it illness, divorce or loss of a job, some with no families or friends to help them out when things are tough. We call these people 40 watts, dim but bright; went through school and university, got institutionalized and now can't see the wood for the trees. Reminds me of most MPs does it not? Take them out of their world and place them in the real one and they are like animals crossing the road!

A wise man once told me when I was young and had just started my own business: "always be good to people on the way up, because you are bound to meet them on the way down". At 20 I never understood fully, still had the world under my feet, and knew it all. Now I understand.

Luckily most people are not like that, and some very rich people are very down to earth, and know how to distribute their wealth. I have been fortunate to have worked for many lords, ladies and famous people when I worked in London and found most very down to earth and easy to talk too.

About 20 years ago, I worked for a Lord who was the adviser to Maggie Thatcher. On calling at his house in Eaton Square London, he gave me his car permit to park outside and said if I was to get a parking ticket it would be ok. Once I parked and unloaded my tools and he made me sit down before I started work as he had made tea and toast, as he was making his own anyway. Different class.

Working in Peppermint Grove in a very posh house, I had cleaned the carpets and was just signing up and talking to the lady, when she asked me where I was from. "UK" I said. "Yes I realised that, but what part?" "London" I said, "and what part are you from?" She had a very well spoken voice. "My dear boy, I was born in Western Australia, and a well educated Australian speaks the Queens English." Well that told me.

Working in some of the richest suburbs of Perth, opens one's eyes to the great divide of wealth and the difference between people, but everyone still has their problems and fears and sadness, just in different degrees. Poorer people might be envious of the rich, but believe me money does not bring you happiness. Love of your family and friends does that, now that is true wealth. As I said before a wise man once told me if you can count the number of true friends on both hands when you die, you would have been a wealthy man.

I have always loved the job and you meet some of the nicest people, young and old along the way. The elderly always want you to sit down and have a cup of tea with them, and have a chat, some show you photos of their family.

One lady in a retirement village always shows me her photos on her sideboard every time I go around there. I've being going there every six months for five years, and every time I go there I say to her "who's that pretty girl in the photo", and she always says to me, "who do you think it is" and I always say "she's very pretty, she looks like you when you must have been younger", and she says it is, "I was only nine when the photo was taken". "Well" I say "you haven't changed a lot I can see it is you". That always puts a smile on her face for the rest of the day I am sure.

We had another elderly lady in Dalkeith, again Jason and myself went to the job as it was booked in for 10 rooms and it is a lot easier to clean big jobs with two of you. Anyway she was showing us around when we went into her bedroom, when she turned around and said it's a long time since I had two men in my bed room. Cheeky cow, only an old lady could get away with that.

One of the most nicest of families you could wish to meet lives in Mosman Park, extremely rich, down to earth, and treats everybody the same. We often talk about new books, travelling, and families.

They are so rich that they bought the house to the side of them, and knocked it down because it blocked their view of the Swan River.

Every 6 months or so I clean their outside patio at a cost of nearly $2,000 because they hold parties.

Another rich family hired me to clean their house in Dalkeith. When I arrived his bodyguard come maintenance man come chauffer showed me around the house as the owners were in their London home, oh they also have a house in Paris. Anyway he said to me would you like to park in the garage and come up through the centre of the house via the underground car park? I said maybe not as I need to open all the doors of my van and might not have enough room. With that he told me I could do a u-turn in it. He was right, and that included the 5 cars that were also parked in the garage: 1 vintage Bentley, 1 vintage Jaguar, an Aston Martin, and two Range Rovers. He said they were probably worth over $1,000,000 all together.

Once in the garage he took me through a side door into a corridor that lit up and turned off as we walked, and we passed a wine cellar the size of a double garage. Inside the cellar were bottles of some vintage wine that I was told were worth tens of thousands, and I believed him, anyone would after what I saw, his table wine they drunk at dinner time was $2,000 a bottle.

Franchise Of The Year!

They actually moaned about the price of sanitizer that I needed to put on a 10 seater lounge suite that had milk stains on. The extra cost of the sanitizer was $80, now she either thought that I was charging her more because they were rich, or they were tight bastards and that was why they were rich.

Now I am not one of those people that believe that all people should have the same, because if you gave 100 people a million dollars and wait to see how they have done two years later, I bet, my million, that 2% would have at least doubled it, 10% would have about the same and the rest would have spent it or have very little left to show for it. Where I would be I don't know but would like to give it a go.

Some people just know how to make money and the rest of us know how to spend it, which sounds like most of our politicians who get a lot of money every year from us taxpayers and waste it on shit. Well if they don't spend their allowance every year, they won't get the same next year to waste, they say. "Well thank fuck for that" most taxpayers would say. It's a shame that top businessmen like Richard Branson don't run our countries as we would be so much better off.

About a year ago while working in a house, an elderly lady, who had lived in Scarborough all her life, told me to read a book by Ken Follett, called The Pillars of Earth, the best book I've ever read she said.

It's about a mason in the 12th century wanting to build a cathedral. Now I am not religious, and nor is the book. It's based in a small town in England during the civil war after the French invasion, and how life was, and really still is between the rich and poor, who are the clever ones, and who were just born into wealth. I have to agree with that lady, little has changed, idiots, not all but many run our country, and are so arrogant that they believe that the people are too uneducated to have their say. We are ok to run small business and employ staff and pay our taxes, to keep them in a job, but not on their level to make the important decisions of life, whatever they are. Anyway enough said on that matter, a carpet cleaner, what does he know?

I was working around an elderly ladies house recently. She was 96 years old, but very active and bright. I went there to clean three rooms and a rug. While I was there she asked me how much to clean her recliner chair, with was very grubby with body oils. She said her daughter asked me to enquire. "Normally it's $89 for one chair, because it is different machinery to clean chairs as it is for carpets, but while I am here I would clean it for $50 if that's ok with you."

She was making a cup of coffee for me at the time. She said "I don't know, I thank you for doing it cheaper, but that still a lot of money to me." "That's ok" I said, "but it needs doing and it will come up really well, but it's up to you."

"I don't know" she said, but as she was walking over with the coffee, she slipped and threw the whole cup of coffee over the chair. We looked at each other, and I said, "I think that just made up your mind". I cleaned the chair.

When she remade me another cup of coffee, I sat down and had a chat with her. I asked when she came to Australia, she said she came over in the late 50's, with her husband and kids, but he walked out after they had been here 10 years, and she brought the kids up on her own. She also said he ran off with his son's Asian girl friend that had lived with them for a year because she was homeless at the time. "Oh" I said "I am sorry". "It's ok" she said, "I was angry then, but when I look back she was ever so pretty, and sexy, so I can see why he did it. My son never forgave him though." "I bet" I said.

I worked in a retirement village in Mt Claremont, and cleaned the carpets of a nice elderly couple, where the majority of villas were occupied by widows. The lady was quite unwell, and her husband was caring for her, as he didn't want to go into a home.

About a year later I was working in another villa next to the couple's one, and asked her how the couple were next door. "Oh she died "she said. "That's a shame, they seemed nice, but she wasn't well when I was there about a year ago."

"She died about three months ago. He's got it made now" she said with a smile, "he gets one of us to do his washing, one or two of us to cook him dinner, one to help with house work, and one to do his ironing. Before she died he was doing it all, but we all felt sorry for him when she died, and he played on it. It annoys some of us." "Not all" I said, "I wonder what favours he does in return?"

Working in the elderly apartments we realise they cannot throw anything away, a lot due to sentimental value, and "because I might need that one day, or I will need to spend some time sorting it all out, but can't find the time". Sometimes there's only about one square metre of carpet left!

Over the years, while working in people's houses, we get asked a lot by customers, especially the ones that are moving, whose parents have died and they are clearing out the house, if we want any of their unwanted items, anything form a vase to a car. I always say no, but Jason the Graymouth Pikey as we all call him, nearly always says yes, he even checks the crap outside the house on bulk rubbish weeks.

He has had two elderly ladies give him old cars, both Gemini's strangely enough. He spent two years and approximately $1,500 on each, doing them up, but gave them away in the end because, he moved, and never finished them off, and didn't want to take them to his new house, because he had nowhere to put them.

Jason and I were offered a hash greenhouse, with all the lights and heaters, which was in a guy's spare bedroom in Scarborough. He had split up from his girl friend, and she reported him to the real estate agent, who was coming around to do a rent inspection, hence we were there to clean the carpets, and he needed to get rid of the green house before the morning, otherwise he would be having the police round. We never took it and don't know who did.

If you were to visit Jason's garage it would be like going into a swap mart.

A couple of Asian ladies we know have tried to get Jason out on blind dates with their friends, because he tells everybody his long time girl friend walked out on him and his small boy.

Not sure if he has gone on any or not, he always says he hasn't, so I have to believe him.

An Italian lady we work for in North Fremantle has some unusual powers. The first time we worked there was on a Saturday. Marinka was with me. She's probably in her mid thirties, married with two children, has a very nice two storey home, she and her husband own a couple of restaurants in Perth. She sometimes helps him out in the restaurants when they are short staffed, but otherwise is a full time mum.

Once we had finished, she made us a cup of coffee, and while drinking it we got on the subject of the paranormal, can't remember why. Maybe John Edwards cross country, was on the television, I really don't know. She told us that she can see auras around people, not all the time, but when she concentrates, they cover the whole body she said.

"What colours are they" I asked, now really interested as I also have had some paranormal experiences in the past. "They are only different shades of white", she said, "it seems to me the nicer the person, may be if I like that person more, the whiter the aura is, if I don't their aura goes almost black."

"How strange" I said, "what do you think an aura is?"

"Well" she said, "I've thought about that a lot over the years, and believe that the aura is your personality, or perhaps your outer soul, like an energy, that moves on when you die, but I really don't know. Some people either don't have one or I just can't see it." Looking at me she said "I can see yours".

"Can you see mine" both me and Marinka said at the same time. She "it's really bright, and white. Stand over here out of the sunshine", and she lead me into the laundry where it was darker. "I can really see it now. It's very white and bright." "Good" I said. Oh yes, well to me anyway.

"Have I got an aura around me" Marinka asked. "Yes as white but not as bright". How strange we thought. I wonder what it really means.

"I know in most children, when I see it, it's always white, maybe because of their age or innocence that they are too young to have done much really wrong. In older people it gets darker. At first I thought it was something to do with how long they have to live, but my grandfather had a very white aura just before he died so it can't be that."

About one year later, just before Christmas, I went around there on my own. It was during the time Marinka had been ill and was in and out of hospital, work was quite slow and we needed a bit of money. Things were just not great.

I cleaned her house ready for Christmas and then after she made me a cup of coffee as usual she said "you have had a hard time of things lately, haven't you?"

"I am ok" I said. I have never liked people knowing I have had problems, don't know why, maybe just male pride.

"I can tell you have had some hard times lately, but don't worry it will all change in the month beginning with M. Don't know whether it's March or May, but one of them. Then everything will be fine, and you will be on the way up again."

Now I have not seen her for over a year, she didn't really know me from a bar of soap, and I have never spoken to her about anything before, as I said I am quite private in that way. I would only talk to people that are really close to me.

"What makes you say that" I asked? "I can sense and feel it" she said. "You might find this odd" she said, "but over the last few weeks two strange meetings happened to people we know. The first was when friends of ours came over for dinner, they brought with them some real estate details of their new house they were going to buy, which looked great."

"As I was reading them, I had a bad feeling that something was wrong with the house. Have you had a full structural survey done?" I asked. "No we haven't because it's only two years old, and looks in perfect condition, apart from some small settlement cracks in the family room, at the back." "Well I would get one" I said. "You sure?" "I would, I can sense something wrong I don't know what, but something." Then my husband said that for the sake of a few hundred dollars it would be worth the peace of mind, and you know, she's not often wrong.

A couple of weeks later they called around, on a Sunday afternoon. They pulled out the house plans, because the survey brought up that the house had been built on a large old soakwell, which was never filled in and the back of the house was slowly moving down. The cracks they saw were originally larger, but had been filled in so as not to look that bad.

She went on: "the second strange feeling I had around the same time was when a friend of my husband brought his new girlfriend around. She was very attractive. They had met a couple of months before, on holiday overseas, where he went with his mates. She was also on holiday with her mates also from Perth."

"When they returned home, they carried on seeing each other, ever since. Now they were planning to get married in a few months. The first time I saw her, I could feel there was something wrong, I went cold and felt odd. I didn't say anything while they were there, but when they left my husband asked 'what's wrong with you, you were rather quiet tonight'."

"I don't like to say this about your friend, but something is not quite right about that girl, she seems nice enough but, there is something not quite right."

"Oh" he said "I don't know what to say, I don't want to upset him, maybe I should just call him in the morning, saying how nice she is, but don't you think it's a bit quick, as you hardly know each other?" "Good idea" she replied.

"A couple of days later, my husband gets a phone call from his mate, before he had spoken to him, saying that he had split up from the girl, because one of his friends had gone around his house, and told him while they were on holiday, he had also slept with his future wife, while he was drunk one night and went to bed early."

"He said he didn't tell him before, because he thought it was just a holiday fling, but he thought he had better own up to what they had done."

I said goodbye to her, and she said "let me know how you got on when I next see you", not really believing all she had said. Maybe she was exaggerating I thought. That night when I got home, I told Marinka all she had said. "Let's hope she's right" she said.

We limped through the next few months, keeping our head above water.

Then in March the hail storm came, generating a lot of work. We had to put on three vans for a long time, which helped pay off our debts. Then in April Marinka had her final radiation treatment, and got the all clear in May.

Also in May, we were still firing at work, and still had three vans on, but one had to have some repairs done, in a body shop in Gnangara. This day the boys were working the vans, but we needed some chemicals that were on the van in Gnangara for repairs, so I went up there first thing in the morning on my motorbike, and picked a five litre container up, just big enough to fit in to the hangar.

As I was driving down the outside lane of Hepburn Avenue at eighty kilometres an hour, which is a two lane dual carriageway, a car pulled out in front of me, and turned right from the other side of the road, causing me to swerve to the inside lane. As I passed her, I gave her the finger and carried on driving until the freeway exit on my left, both still two lanes. As I slowed down to take the exit onto the freeway, the same car that had pulled out in front of me, took the exit too fast on the outside lane, and drove right in to me.

As I braked and stopped, the car ran alongside me, hitting my elbow and foot, until it stopped in front of me. I went mad at her, telling her she could have killed me. She tried to say I was changing lanes, and that she worked for an insurance company, and it was my fault, until two people came over from the train station car park, having witnessed what had happened, and gave me their phone numbers. They both couldn't believe that me and the bike were still standing, and even more unbelievable was that she had two large indents down both top and bottom of her doors and wings, where she caught both my elbow and foot. I was unhurt and the bike untouched.

When the insurance company rang me up a couple of weeks later, asking how much damage I had to my bike, and I said none. They couldn't believe that I was untouched, but she had $5,000 worth of damage to her car. Incredible.

December that same year I returned to the Italian lady's house, ready for Christmas. She greeted me at the door, and said "you look and feel good". "I do" I said, "thanks".

"How's things been with you?"

"Good" I said "you were right things did change for the better, but it was between March and May" and I explained all that had happened. She said "good. I could see it. Also you must have a guardian angel looking after you."

"Funny you should say that, lots of my friends and sisters tell me that, as I should have died about six or seven times."

I explained about the other near death experiences I've had. I have fallen from two roofs, once landing on a motorbike when I was seventeen, rushed to hospital in an ambulance, being let out after seeing the doctor saying I was fitter then him.

The second time I was working four stories high, when the wind pushed me. As I was rolling down the roof to a sure death, I hit a

37

chimney stack at the bottom of the roof. I laid there shaking till help came, and got me down.

I've had another two near misses on motor bikes, one when driving at dusk about a hundred kms per hour when a six foot Kangaroo came running out of the bush, but suddenly stopped to let me pass. I can still see his face as I drove by braking. The other one was when I was driving in England, down a country lane at about seventy miles an hour, when a pigeon flew at me the other way. I just ducked in time, and it took a large chunk out of my helmet, better than going through my visor, and certain death.

The last and strangest was when I was diving in a large lake in Nottingham, England. It was a cold day in summer, only my seventh or eighth dive. I was doing my advance Padi. The first time I had worn a full wet suit and used a steel oxygen bottle. Six of us jumped in the lake. It was cold, dark and 120 meters deep. At the bottom lay a submarine.

As we jumped in I was at the back, so last in. On entry my left hand fin came off, the others had swum away, so I was left to retrieve the fin on my own. As you may know, you need your fins to swim underwater with all the scuba gear on. As I was going down, I caught the other fin on a rocky shelf, thus knocking the other fin off, and with that I went into panic mode, forgetting to equalise my BCD, and started to sink fast down the black hole towards the submarine. Now I am really panicking, got really hot and all I wanted to do was take my mask off and the regulator out my mouth.

When all of a sudden, out from nowhere this other diver grabbed hold of me, stared into my eyes, through two pairs of masks, I can still see these eyes today. When all of a sudden I was rushing to the top, seeing light, as they must have took my weight belt off. I remember floating on the top thinking I am never going down there again as I lay looking up at the sky. I did carry on and became a dive master, but at that time I believed in God, and was going to become a land animal only.

I never knew how they saved me, I tried to find out all day in between dives, without luck.

"As I said you have a guardian angel with you, I can sense it. Have you ever sensed somebody with you ever?"

"Now you say that I have had quite a few super natural experiences throughout my life, but that's a long story, and I haven't got time to tell you now, but if you want I will next time, but thanks for your help."

"It wasn't me that helped you, I could only sense and feel what was going to happen, it was you."

A real estate friend of mine asked me to quote for a large tile and grout clean at a three story house in Quinns Rocks. Nice quite modern house one street up from the beach.

The bank had repossessed the house from the owners that had built it a couple of years back, using the top floor as their residence, the two floors below as bed and breakfast apartments, the ground floor one big garage and store room.

I went around there one evening, while it was still light. I lived at the time ten minutes away.

Meet her there, she told me "the banks want a price to clean all the floors, before they put it on the market, so have a look around and let me know, I need to wait here for a electrician."

I went up to the top floor, which felt quite cold, for a hot summer's day in Perth, then quickly checked all the floors to see the extent of work to price.

With pen, paper and tape I went back up to the top floor and realized how cold it was again, started measuring the size of the rooms, when I felt somebody following me, at first I thought it was the real estate agent, but looking out the window, I saw her still waiting by her car.

So I went back to measuring the room sizes, this time the feeling was really strong that somebody was behind me watching me. All the hairs on my arms and back of my neck, started to stand up, I got colder, and didn't feel good at all. Similar experiences have happened to me before, but not like this. I quickly looked around the rest of the floor, and guessed the size and got out of the door leading down as quickly as possible. As soon as I was outside it stopped, I felt warm again, my hairs went down, no more bad feeling. It changed in an instant.

Measured the rest of the floors and went to find the real estate agent. She was still waiting for me, by her car. "Still no electrician?" I asked. "No not yet, he has still got ten minutes before he is late." "You could have come up with me."

"No I when up to the top yesterday I didn't feel very good, that's why I stayed down here."

"That's funny" I said and told her what had happened to me. "Yes that's it", she said. I looked into it afterwards and found out that the owners husband died on a boat trip, while fishing, just after they finished building the place, his coffin was on that floor, that's when the lift was working, I was wondering why the lift never worked. By all accounts it stopped working that day, they had to carry him down, and it never worked since.

They say a workman died working on the lift when they installed it and he got crushed at the bottom. Then shortly afterwards, his wife went bankrupt. Not a lucky house then.

"No, I am not looking forward to showing people around it." "And I am not looking forward to cleaning it" I said.

When I got home I told Marinka the story, and said I am going to double the price, and if I get it I am going to sub it out. I am not going back. Learnt some other facts about that house, but don't know if they are true, and don't care.

Blood, Urine, and Wine

My least favourite jobs are wee, poo and blood extraction, followed by water damage cause by flooding.

Wee and poo accidents are not only caused by the elderly and sick, as you might think. I have had to clean two mattress in a hotel, where a group of lads had gone out on the lash, got so pissed that they booked a room for the night, or pre-booked it knowing they were going to get pissed, fallen asleep, and one of them had pissed the bed. Unbelievable? Don't think so.

I have had elderly folk, obviously not very well, because most are so embarrassed when I get there and they have to tell me what had happened. They have accidents almost everywhere. Most just fall into a deep sleep or it comes on too quickly, and then it's too late. I have had poo and wee on lounge suites, beds, and carpets. Health and my safety is my biggest concern in all those cases.

Blood is another problem of not only the elderly, but mainly, as lots of them are on blood thinners, and if they just knock themselves, they bleed like a pig.

The worst blood job was when a guy got so pissed at a party, he ran through a glass patio door. Blood was everywhere and I don't know how he didn't die. He nearly cut his arm off.

Dog and cat piss and poo are very common also. Maltese shiatsu's being the worst for some reason, we call them Maltese Pisswhos. A guy in a big house in Mosman Park, whose paintings were on the walls and statues all over the place, must have been worth more than most people's home, had six of them just running around his house, when you walked in you could just smell ammonia everywhere, and I can't believe he couldn't smell it, perhaps being just used to it.

The only reason he was getting his carpets cleaned because he was having family from overseas to stay. He had more dog wee than carpet, what made it worse it was all up the stairs also. We had to dual clean and sanitise the whole upstairs, including the stairs. His rugs downstairs needed cleaning as they covered the wooden floors, but he said he didn't think they were that bad, but they were disgusting.

A lot of dog owners can't smell their dogs, but as soon as we walk into a house, we know if they have a dog or not.

One of my customers called me one day, because she had a bad smell in her bedroom. She told me she believed it to be her mother's dog, who she was dog sitting for, and that it must have got into the bedroom and peed. We took everything out off the room, extracted and then dry cleaned the carpet, and sanitised the whole carpet.

Two days later, she calls me back, still with the same smell, so I cleaned and sanitised it again.

I never heard no more, until I went around there a couple of years later, to clean the whole house. I asked her, "do you remember the bad smell in your bedroom, and I had to clean it twice?"

"Yes" she said, "do you know what that was, it was a dead rat in the roof. We forgot that we had put poison in the loft, and it wasn't until we saw a damp patch on the ceiling that we called a roofer, because we thought we had a leak, and that is how he found the dead rat."

"The smell was horrendous." I remembered.

There have been so many dog wee and poo jobs it's hard to remember them all, only the worst ones.

We have had some bad experiences with the elderly, where they have pissed or pooed on the floor or upholstery, where they have fallen asleep or been ill, and haven't got to the toilet on time.

We got called out to one emergency job, where this ladies mum had got ill in the night and went into a semi-coma sitting in her brand new electric recliner they had bought that weekend. She had bled through her back passage. When her daughter found her they thought she was dead, but luckily she was rushed to hospital and survived.

We were left to clean up the mess. Normally I would have walked away from a job like that, and told them to buy a new chair, which is not cheap. Her daughter was so nice, and under a lot of stress, that I decided to clean it, plus I got well paid for it. It came up good.

We have had jobs where the elderly have fallen over and cut themselves and where they are on blood thinning drugs, bleeding everywhere. Mind you we also had a job where a young man got so drunk, he walked through a patio door, and cut himself to pieces. He also survived.

There are many reasons why people have their carpets, upholstery etc cleaned: rent inspections, dogs or animals fouling them, so bad they have to, this type usually expect miracles, and as we say these are hands and not wands. Some clean their belongings regularly, most when they have to.

We have one lady who lives in a nice house in Nedlands, with lots of French furnishings that we clean for quite regularly. The first time I cleaned her house she had about 8 rabbits loose in the house pooing and weeing everywhere, with hair stuck in the carpet. I cleaned the carpets and rugs and sanitized the lot and when walking out I felt disgustingly dirty and needed a shower. I swore blind I would never work there again. One year later she calls me up to clean her carpets etc again, I asked if she still had her rabbits and she told me that some of them had died and the last two were now in a rabbit pen in the garden. Ok I thought, that's ok and arranged a time and date to do her job. She was right she didn't have rabbits, she now had about 6 indoor cats, pissing and pooing on the carpet with more hair then any rabbits.

Now when she calls I still take the job, but I get one of my employees to go around there, I have done my bit.

Water damage from flooding is also a pain to do, most the jobs I have done are due to washing machines waste hoses becoming detached, or splitting. The next most common one is fish tanks busting, now the smell is not very nice either, smells like stagnant water, worse than poo I think.

Also it's an expensive job for them if they haven't got insurance, and most of the time if they have the excess is so high it just covers the cost of drying, cleaning and sanitising the carpets, apart from the inconvenience, as it's done over a few days, due to the drying process.

Mind you they are pleased when it's over and their carpets are back to what they are.

Some people try to get us to say it was worse than what it was, to get more out of the insurance company, and as I say to them, if you want someone to lie for you, you are best to get another company, because it's not worth me losing my business for the sake for a couple of hundred dollars.

I have never had anyone say they didn't want us to do the job; maybe they saw the sense in what I was saying or were too embarrassed. Don't know.

The funniest call out was from a previous customer, that I had worked for many a time. A really lovely South African lady, who comes across very harsh in her mannerisms, maybe due to her accent, but when you get to know her she is one of the nicest people you could meet.

She called me at 9.30 one Sunday morning, apologising for such a call on a Sunday, but her dogs had had an accident on her carpets, in both the lounge and her bedroom, and it was diarrhoea.

What had happened was she had been working 10-14 hour shifts at the hospital, where she works as a surgeon. She got home late at night and let the dogs in, and then fell asleep on the sofa, forgetting to let them out again, being outside dogs. So they must have had upset tummies, but she was so tired she slept through it, not knowing until her son woke her up in the morning.

I went around there first thing Monday morning, as now the damage was done. Depending on age, sex, if they are pregnant, and what they eat, would determine how well the carpet would clean and if there would be any staining. The body acids would determine that, and depending on the above they can change very quickly.

Also this was not a cheap job, as we had to sanitise first, then steam clean and suck all the poo out of the carpet, before we could dry clean and then dry clean and sanitise again, and finally clean our equipment. Two of us were there three hours at a cost of $500. Cheap considering we saved her carpets without a mark on them.

Then two days later she called me up again, this time quite angrily, telling me the dogs had done it again, this time she had gone to bed early as it was now her time off, but her son had come home late, probably drunk, let the fucking dogs in, forgot about them and the fucker went to bed. She woke up to find they had shit all over the place again, her words not mine, and in the same places. Well the air was blue, she had calmed down a bit when I arrived, but was still angry. He's paying for this, this time she said. Another $500 later we left. I have been back a few times since and now she laughs about it.

I still get my cup of coffee and toast, hot cross buns at Easter, every time I go there, and she always tells me off if I am late, like I am a naughty boy, but she's a great lady and always asks after Marinka and the kids.

I have had to clean both lounge suites and mattresses where people have let their cats give birth to a litter, couldn't believe it.

The most common mattress clean is where babies have wet the bed, in some cases before their husbands find out, as they have let them sleep in their bed.

One Hotel I work for has called me out on several occasions to clean the mattresses, on a Monday morning where a group of lads had booked the room for the week-end and one of them had got so drunk he wet the bed. Sad!

On two occasions I have cleaned the mattresses due to ladies taking their dogs in the room and they have wet the bed.

I had one poor lady call in an emergency, saying her 6 year old daughter had come into her bedroom in the morning, and was just sick everywhere. When I got there I couldn't believe the amount of

45

vomit that had come out of a really skinny little 6 year old Indian girl. It looked like somebody had emptied a bath.

Red wine is another common emergency call out. I have had a number of strange jobs to do in that department. Most of them involving the opposite sex funnily enough.

The first one was when I just started out. A guy called me up in a panic that he had spilt a glass of red wine on his white shag pile rug, quite ironic I suppose.

When I got around there he explained that his girl friend had gone away for a few days, and he told me he had had a party while she had gone, and that someone had knocked over a glass of red wine. Well not the end of the world I said, it could happen to anyone. Well not really he said they didn't drink red wine nor does any of his mates, and she's coming back in the morning and mustn't see it otherwise his life would not be worth living. "Like that?" I said "hope she was worth it." "It was at the time" he said. I saved his bacon that day.

Another funny occasion was when a lady called me to clean the red wine off her in her bedroom, she had got drunk over the weekend and brought a man home, took red wine to bed and both got carried away and her leg knocked over the wine glass, bit too much information to tell me, but my mind could see the whole accident happening, not that I could see him that well, or maybe it was another girl, I would be able to see that better. Some people tell you the strangest things, maybe I should stop asking.

I had a young lad about 18 ring me up early on a Saturday morning in a complete panic, I had worked for his parents on a few occasions, but they had gone on holiday and left him in charge of the house while they were away, not one of their better ideas I am sure.

Anyway, he had had a party the night before, and someone had dropped a full casket of red wine at the top of the stairs which bounced and burst half way down the stairs, spilling red wine all down the lower half, up the wall, and on to the hallway carpet.

We did a poo job for nothing one day.

Marinka came out with me that day because we were really busy, so she helped me vacuum while she was taking the bookings on the run.

We were working in a very nice two story house in City Beach, for a previous customer, we also do her offices.

She's a very fussy customer but extremely nice at the same time. The work was on the first floor, so you had to go through the garage, up a flight of stairs to get there. I was bringing up the rest of the equipment while Marinka started to vacuum the theatre room. I just got up the stairs, when I heard the lady saying to Marinka "what's all that on my carpets?" "I don't know" Marinka said, "but it looks like dog poo." As she said that she looked on her shoe and she had shit all on both soles of her shoes. "Oh I am really sorry" she said "I will get Peter to sort it out." "You better" she said.

Marinka had walked dog poo, all up the stairs, along the hall and into the theatre room.

"I am sorry" I said, "I will sort it out straight away, we can extract it and sanitise it, and you will never know it was there."

"Are you sure" she said "it won't leave a mark or smell?" "I promise you if it does I will pay to replace the carpets. As it will be done straight away, it will be easy to be removed."

"I hope so" she said. "It's a promise."

Marinka was so upset that the lady said to her "don't worry about it you didn't mean it, and if Peter can clean it up, it will be fine."

All was good and we still clean her house and surgery.

March Storms 2010

During the hailstorms in March 2010, we were at our busiest as we also do water damage and restoration work. We spent the first two days drying and cleaning carpets, upholstery, rugs, etc, then the next two weeks ripping them out.

The hailstones that day were the size of golf balls, and the wind gale force. It only lasted for about two downpours of about 30 minutes each time, but boy did it cause some damage.

I was picking up Michael, Marinka's son, from school, when the heavens opened the first time, and we were stuck in a traffic jam, watching the downpour. The C of a Coles sign came flying down the road over the top of us, cars were getting stuck at roundabouts where the roads turned into rivers, we were fortunate that we were higher up in the van.

When I got home I checked the van's paint work, not a mark on it. Shortly after, the second storm hit us, but this time I watched it from inside, drinking a cup of coffee.

When Marinka got home from work, the storms had passed. Her car had been in the car park where she worked and on inspecting the paint work on the car we found it was covered in dents all down one side, the roof and bonnet.

We had so many phone calls over the next few weeks that we couldn't cope even with 3 vans on the road, because we still had our normal booked jobs, plus all the flood damage work coming in. We were working flat out.

After the first 48 hours the insurance companies instructed by the government, realised that all the water restoration companies couldn't cope and that if they didn't start just ripping out the wet carpets they would have a bigger problem on their hands, Bactria.

One of the jobs we were called out to was some offices that had been flooded a week prior to us getting there. The office had been cleared of furniture, so we started to rip the carpets out on the first floor. The first two offices were easy, as they were laid on underlay, but the last one was carpet tiles which were stuck down.

There were about 50 square meters, so I went down to the local hardware shop and bought two spades to prize them up. It took both of us three hours by the time we stacked them and took them downstairs.

At the end of the job my right shoulder was killing me, and the next day, even worse.

I carried on working, at a slower pace I might add, because we were still flat out. In the mean time, that weekend I helped my daughter Carly move house.

After a couple of weeks when things died down, my shoulder was still hurting. I decided to go to physiotherapist to try to sort it out. Two weeks and four sessions later he sent me for an x-ray where they told me I need a cortisone injection, which I had done. Good for about two days, then had to go back to the doctors, who then sent me to a specialist, who sent me for a scan which showed that I had ripped the muscles off the bone, so I needed an operation.

One week later, I was in hospital have a shoulder reconstruction. They had to put a plate into my bone to attach the muscles, but also had to scrape some atherosclerosis from the bone.

Marinka drove me there early one Tuesday morning. I had the operation at about 10 o'clock, work up about 2 o'clock coming in and out of consciousness, by 3 o'clock I remember waking up properly, shoulder strapped up, with a pain killer feed in my arm, for the pain, of which I had none for some reason.

When a nurse came in I asked her if I could go outside for a cigarette, as I was gasping for one. "No" she said "you have only just come out of the operating room."

"Great" I said "when can I go home?"

"How's your pain" she asked. "I haven't got any" I said.

"So" she said "how much of the pain killer have you used?"

"None" I said, "I am not in pain. No sense on feeling."

She checked, and said "you're right; I will ask the doctor if he will allow you to go home."

"Thanks I would rather go home and rest in my own bed than sleep here." Off out she went to ask the doctor. In the meantime an orderly came in and brought some tea and sandwiches which we eat, Marinka fussing too much, thinking I must be in more pain than I was. About an hour later the nurse came back, and said "the doctor said if you still haven't had any pain killers by 5 o'clock and aren't in pain I could discharge myself."

Had to wait that long just in case the drugs they gave me when I had the operation were still working, even though they should have worn off an hour ago. She checked the pain killer count again and realised I still hadn't used it. An hour later we were walking out the hospital. We had to go to a chemist for pain killers and anti-inflammatories just in case I needed them that night.

Never ever used them, my shoulder was never in pain fully, unless I stretched too much, when it was more uncomfortable.

Was off manual work for 6 weeks, just took the phone calls, doing the bookings and paperwork. The boys had to do the manual work. I wasn't able to drive for 8 weeks and should have been off manual labour for three months, but one of the boys started to muck me about, so I had to sack him, and we were so busy at the time, that I had to go back to work early, Marinka was not pleased, but that is the joys of running your own business.

Kept doing the exercises the doctor told me to do, which helped enormously. Six months later I was back playing golf, one year later nearly back to normal, and we are still going to insurance jobs due to that storm.

I had one unpleasant, if not strange experience during that month. I was called out by a real estate agent that we do a lot of work for throughout the year, to look at a house in Nedlands, which was a particularly badly hit area. When I got to the house, I noticed the builder was there, repairing all the lead lighted windows with plastic sheets, which the hail had smashed. The builder was the property managers' husband. He showed me the damaged carpets, where the rain had come through, the broken windows, and said the tenants didn't want us to be there, while they were at work, but the owners did, otherwise the damage could get worse, so they had to repair the window, and dry the carpet today. I had a quick look around, and found the carpets dry, just covered with glass, and dirty. Told the builder I would be back later when he had finished. I agreed to pick the keys up from the agent, later that same day, and left.

I picked the keys up later that day and went to the house, the two big iron gates were shut this time, pulled up, opened them, and drove into the carport, went around the side and opened the side door, rung the bell to check if anybody was in, waited, then unlocked the door. Looked around to check what I had to do again. The builder had removed all the large pieces of glass which was good. Went back to the van and started to unload. As I was unloading a boy on a bike was at the gates looking in, I said hi, didn't really take much notice of him at the time, except he was on a bike, had a school uniform on, and had a school bag on his back. He rode off and I went in the house, vacuumed, cleaned and sanitised the carpets, replaced all the equipment back into the van, and went over to the Deli on the corner to get a coffee to take away for the drive home. It was now about 4.30 pm.

Returning to the van a saw a car parked behind my van, thought some other company was checking for damage. Went over to see them when this man gets out the car, and said to me without saying hello, "what are you doing here, you have no right being on my property." "Who are you" I asked. "We live here and you have no right being here when we are not a home."

Franchise Of The Year!

"You're the tenant are you? Well the real estate agent gave me the key and asked me to clean the carpets now, to stop any further damage. As far as I am concerned, that's all I know, you need to speak to the real estate agent, I will call them now." I went to van to call the agent. As I got to the van and start to call the agent this woman, for the want of a better word, came around the corner shouting at me that "I told them not to fucking come in my house, when we are not here". "It's not your house" I said, "you're just renting it, we need to clean it quickly, to be safe and clean, what's your problem? Talk to the agent."

I handed her the phone, and I could hear every word she was saying. This nutty woman started shouting at me that I was a fucking paedophile; I was in the house while a minor was there. With that, now angry, I got out of the van, and started to walk around to see her, and said "if you don't shut up now, you stupid woman I am going to slap you".

Her husband started to come towards me, and I looked at him and said, "if you don't shut her up, or come any closer to me I am going to knock you out as well, so just move the your car, to let me get going home."

He backed off, said he had called the police and I needed to wait for them as they were on their way. Still on the phone I said to the real estate agent "can you hear this?" "Yes" she said, "I am on my around there to see you." "Great" I said.

A large crowd had formed now, outside the deli and over the road watching all of us. She was still walking up and down shouting some crap. By now I had calmed down, was sitting in my van with the music on and drinking my coffee when the police arrived.

They took a statement from the tenants and a statement from me. I told them exactly what had happened and that nobody was in the house, but this boy was at the gate. I now know it was their son, and he must have gone to one of his parents and told them I was at their house.

They just said she was hysterical, and needed to talk to her again, the owners of the real estate arrived and gave the police a statement, apologised to me for the inconvenience it had caused. The tenants were told to leave. I backed out and went home, still not really believing all that had just happened. I only went there to clean the carpets.

For the next few weeks after, any time I worked for the real estate company, I was known as paedophile Pete!

Sexy Stories

Jason and I would often send photos of unusual things in people's houses to each other i.e. large dogs, vibrators under beds, sexy girls in photos, fetish photos, cloths all over the floor, really dirty houses, and the list goes on.

Talking of vibrators, I went into this house early one morning in North Fremantle that I have been around to many times before. It's a Doctor who is separated from his wife, and is renting there. Sometimes when I go his children are there, other times when they are not, there's a new girlfriend. I must admit he has good taste, or all his nursing staff are lookers.

Anyway this time he was there with his new girlfriend, another looker who opened the door with little left to the imagination. "Oh shit" she said "we got up late for work." I wonder why I was thinking, I would have stayed in bed longer too if I was him, anyway she asked if I could wait a minute, so I did. When Doc came out, he was all apologetic, as he wanted me to get there earlier, because he had an early start.

"Never mind" I said, "by the time I get the equipment off the van and set up you will probably be ready", and off he went to get ready.

Ten minutes later he was jumping in his car after leaving me his credit card details, and it was alright to make a start as she was now decent.

In I go, now we move what we can off the carpets, then vacuum first and then clean and sanitise if they want, depending on the pile of the carpet rake as well, to help dry and bring the pile up. We always start at the most distant room and work our way out to the front door.

She was now ready, but rushing about, said good-bye and out she went.

I went into their bedroom and started to lift small items off the floor ready to vacuum when I saw the large black vibrator standing upright on the bedside cabinet. Now I was in a quandary, because I had to move the bedside cabinet, and when doing so it would have fallen

54

over anyway, so I took a photo of it and sent it to Jason, then decided the best thing to do was to open the top draw and drop it in, which is what I did. Hoping that she forgot what she had done with it, realised she must have put it away.

Well I had put it into the draw and moved the bedside cabinet into the ensuite, when I heard the front door open and the girl come running into the bedroom, we both looked at each other, and she said "did I leave any anything on the bedside cabinet?" "You did" I said, "but I thought it best to put it away, just in case the kids come back later, it's in your top draw." "Thanks" she said and goodbye and went back out. I carried on smiling.

The other great vibrator story is when both Jason and I went to a job that we had been to a few times before, used to go every six months just before the rent inspection.

This time we had both carpets and upholstery, hence both of us doing the job, Jason was cleaning the carpets in the rear of the house, while I was cleaning the lounge suite in the front room.

I went out to see the lady, to ask if she wanted to sanitize the lounge suite as it was covered in baby milk and vomit, and really needed to be sanitised to kill all the germs.

She was sitting at her dining room table, working on the computer. They seemed a nice family, emigrated over to Australia a couple of years back from Nottingham, England, both working, her part time as she now had a baby. Had a chat with her, and noticed she had an adult toy box to the right of her, never took much notice at the time, and went back to clean the lounge suite.

Jason finished first, then he packed away his gear on to the van and started to write up the invoice while sitting next to the lady. When all of a sudden I heard Jason call out "Peter, Peter you must come here and see this!" She was saying "no don't show Peter, any way it's not for me it's for my husband", and with that she took the adult box that contained a strap on dildo and hid it in her bedroom.

I apologised for Jason while smiling to myself, wondering what she meant by it being for her husband, many options I suppose, tried not to think too deep about that one. Well we signed up and said good-bye and left thinking we won't be back there, but I can be wrong. We still go back two days before a rent inspection. Nothing more was ever said about the strap on, but every time we talk about her we always call her strap on.

When we first started, I went around a ladies house in Wembley Downs, nice but quite an old house, on a hill.

The lady seemed nice but very fussy, had to move everything, checked as I was doing it, now starting to drive me mad, when I said something, she said "the last carpet cleaner didn't do a good job". "I see" I said. "Now I understand you need to trust me first."

With that she asked me if I wanted a cup of tea, great I said, more to get her out the way.

Ten minutes later she called me, to say my tea was on the front porch, on the patio table. Thanks I said, and went out to get it. When I got there, her husband was sitting down at the table. He had been tidying the front garden, and was having a rest also.

On the table was two trays, each with a cup and saucer, tea pot, strainer, jug of milk, pot of sugar, two spoons, plate of sandwiches cut in triangles, and a piece of cake.

Sitting down I looked at him and said hi, he must have read the expression on my face, because he said "I know, I've lived with it all my life, she has to do everything perfect, but her heart is in the right place." "I can see that" I said, "it could be a lot worse". "I know that" he said.

We chatted about this and that for fifteen minutes while drinking our tea, with our little finger sticking out, just in case she was watching us.

When I finished I thanked her, and she said, "no thank you, I had cleaned the rest of the house yesterday, all the carpets and rugs look great, only the garden to get finished."

"Spring clean or party" I asked. "Oh no, my women's group are coming over tomorrow, and I just wanted to tidy the house. We take it in turns every so many months and it's my turn. Their houses are always spick and span, I don't want to let the side down."

"Good" I said, "I don't think you will," and left.

Every so many months from the day, I have gone around there, just cleaning the downstairs as her ladies never go up stairs.

Since then she has moved to a smaller house, on one floor. Her husband is now not very well, and shakes a lot spilling his drinks and food, which annoys the hell out of her, but she looks after him very well. I still go around the new house every so often, and clean the carpets and also the chair he sits on, ready for ladies day. She gets her daughter to take her husband out for the day as otherwise it would be too much hard work she says.

Her nick name is Mrs. Bouquet, (Mrs. Bucket) as if you hadn't guessed.

Jason and I used to have some laughs together quite often, but, also he could embarrass me due to his bluntness. He was not the sharpest tool in the box, and would be the first to admit it to you. That's what I liked about him, he was what he was, no bull shit there, but sometimes I found him embarrassing to say the least, this was one of those times.

We were working together again this day, and our 13:30 job was in Scarborough. When we arrived, and she opened the door I knew straight away that I was going to have a problem with Jason. She was young, not many clothes on, and those that she did have on didn't leave much to the imagination, also she was a Kiwi from a town not far from him on the South Island in New Zealand. Bad combination, not only was she good to look at, he now had a reason to keep looking while he chatted to her about back home etc.

She showed us what she wanted done, with Jason in tow like a puppy dog, asking her a thousand and one questions. I decided to get the equipment in while he helped her move bits off the carpet.

When I came back in with the gear I heard her say do you mind if I go to the toilet, he got into a fluster, and went all red. He had been following her everywhere, even into the loo. When she came out I apologised for him, as I had already told him to leave her alone, and get on with his work, but he couldn't see what he was doing wrong he just thought he was being friendly. "I think he fancies you" I said. "Really?" she replied, "do you think?"

He's done similar things many times, but that was the worst, he just doesn't realise he becomes a pest, he really believed he was just being friendly.

A man rang me up to book in to clean his carpets in Wembley Downs. When arriving at the house, an Asian lady let me in and showed me what they wanted done. Looking around the house I decided that some of the rooms needed sanitizing due to food and drink stains.

I spoke to the lady, who was in the kitchen with a man I presumed to be her husband. I explained to them that they needed some extra work done, how much and did they want me to carry on, when she said you need to ask my husband, who was at work. The man in the kitchen I presume was a family friend. I went outside to the van, called her husband, and he paid the bill with his credit card over the phone.

I unloaded my equipment and started to take it all into the house, on going in I explained that I had spoken to her husband and he agreed to carry on. She asked me how long I would be, I said about 45 minutes, and she said she would get out of the way and sit in the garden.

Cleaned and sanitized the carpets, packed the equipment back in the van, and went to find her in the garden.

Well I found her sitting with her skirt up, on the guys lap on a dining room chair! She had her back to me moving up and down. He was looking straight at me, then looked away. She stopped moving but for the obvious reason couldn't get off, I just said I've finished now and your husband paid over the phone with credit card details, walked up to them and left the invoice on the table next to them. Neither of them said a word, just nodded. I said good-bye and left.

Women tell you about their husbands and partners, some same sex, whether they are working away or not, some quite happy that they are working away, so they can do what they want when they want. And get annoyed when they are back home for a week or two, bloody under my feet as they say.

One lady told me she had just separated from her husband because she found him in bed with his best mate. She had come home a day earlier, from visiting her relatives down south, and thought she would surprise him by getting home early. She said she didn't know who was the most surprised, him, her or the boyfriend. She also added she was quite annoyed as she had always fancied his mate as well. I always wondered about him when I think back now. She said he was never that affectionate, or really interested in sex, but I just thought he had a low sex drive, now I know why. We keep in touch because of the kids, as she had three kids. "Well he must have been fairly interested to have three kids", what else do I say to that conversation. "I think it might have been when we were drunk" she said. "Well how long had you been together?" I asked. "Eight years." "Well that's a long time not to have known, didn't you realize when he use to wear your clothes when you were out", I said joking. "He told me all men do that" she quickly replied.

Another lady on my first visit to her house was even more direct. While I was unloading the equipment from the van, she made me a cup of coffee, once made, she said have your coffee, Blazing Saddles is on television, you can watch with me if you like. Well not to seem rude I sat down on the same lounge suite as her, there was only one and no chair.

Then she started to tell me about her life. She said she was married with a girl, well this seemed odd as she was living in a Homeswest home on her own, anyway I carried on listening to her and she carried on by telling me her husband used to abuse her and her daughter when she was younger. The daughter by all accounts was now 14 years old and lives with the father, because she had a car accident and nearly died, was in hospital with head injuries, which sometimes gave her fits. It was all beginning to make sense now, she was a nutter!

Then all of a sudden she said to me "I haven't had sex for years, not since the accident, and the only time I come is when I masturbate." "Ok" I said, not knowing how to answer that, "I'd better carry on or I will be late for my next job", got up and carried on cleaning the carpets.

When I finished, I signed up, thanked her for the coffee, and started to leave, when she said if ever you are in the area pop in any time for coffee. Thanks I said. Three hopes!

Had an early call to a job, 7:30 am, she told me the keys would be in the meter box and money on the kitchen bench as she had to go to work and nobody would be home.

Pulled up onto the drive, got out, got key from meter box, opened door, just about to walk in, when I noticed a girl lying on top of a sleeping bag. It was the middle of summer, the television was on. She just had a T-shirt on, which was rising to show her bare bum. I slowly backed out, slowly closing the door behind me, trying to be really quiet, so as not to disturb her, or let her know I had seen her. I then took a deep breath, and banged on the door, and waited. After a couple of minutes, she opened the door, still only wearing the T shirt.

"Hi" I said, "I have come to clean the carpets, didn't think anybody would be home."

"No" said this really pretty and attractive young girl of about 25 years old, "I came home a day early from down south, but got home late last night. I am her flatmate, I knew you were coming though, but I just woke up when you knocked, I am knackered."

"If you like" I said "I will give you ten minutes, to sort yourself out, while I unload the van."

"Great" she said, "I am making some coffee do you want one?" "Great white with one sugar."

I let her go back inside and started to unload all the equipment. Gave her another knock on the door, she said come in, so in I went. She had put the sleeping bag away, the television was still on, and she was in the kitchen, still only with her T-shirt on. This is going to be a good day I was thinking to myself. "Here's your coffee" she said, passing it to me. As she said it her nipples where poking so far out, I thought they were going to poke me in the eye, door stops comes to mind. I tried to not make it obvious that I was looking at her, but not sure I achieved my goal.

I put my coffee down on the kitchen work top, and thought I had better be professional here and do some work. Checked with her what needed to be done. "Both bedrooms, the lounge, dining room and hall" she said, "I will help you move some of the stuff off the floor." "What do you want moved?" "I will move the big stuff, if you can get your personal bits off the bedroom floors" I said. It was great just watching her move around the house, with very little on. Once we finished tidying up, she sat cross legged on the sofa, and I vacuumed all the carpets, spent most of the time in the lounge where she was sitting, trying hard not to look at her fanny. I don't know why some girls do that, what they do, maybe they don't realise, what they are doing, or are just prick teasers, or get off on it I don't know, but bring it on. It's doesn't upset me.

She didn't move from the sofa all the time I was there, I finished the clean, wrote out the invoice and left it on the side, picked up my money and said goodbye, putting that down to one of my better jobs, you always remember them.

Got a call early one morning from a regular customer of mine, explaining that she was getting a Ikea television cabinet being delivered the next day, being Friday, and was going to make it up over the weekend, was there any chance I could pop around and clean the carpet where the new cabinet was going, and come back and clean the rest of the carpet once they had finished fixing it?

I went around that afternoon. She opened the door and I noticed she was as sexy as ever wearing a T-shirt and quite a short skirt. Had a quick chat as I had known her for at least 5 years, cleaned her old house before she had children, seen her pregnant both times and now her children were at school and kindy.

She explained what she wanted done, the carpet where the unit was going cleaned and sanitised, as the dog liked to sleep in that area. The rest later. Done as instructed, when I was finished, she said staring at me "let's book the next visit", and then she said "you've got really sexy eyes, haven't you?" "Have I", I said. "You know you have" she said. "Thanks", what do you say to that?

She then shook her head and said, "right what day?" "What's the best day for you?" I said, "when will you be finished?" "We will have it done by Monday, but would rather wait to the Thursday, when my husband can take the kids and dog out, and I will be on my own, giving the carpets a chance to dry better." "Ok" I said and said my goodbyes. When I went back I took one of the boys, just in case.

When we had both franchises, we had, one Saturday, a job in Como. Being a Saturday, Marinka was helping that day. Our first job was a large house, four bedrooms at the back, with a hall, large family room, dining room, study, formal lounge, another hall, and master bedroom. A Japanese lady let us in. She was the only occupant that day. She showed us around and we started.

Marinka vacuumed the rooms, starting at the back of the house working our way to the front then out the door, back into the van, good system. I followed behind her bonnet cleaning the carpets, then, Marinka writes up the invoice, while I rake. We both tidy up.

I was on the last room but one, the master bedroom. I always use the socket in the ensuite to plug my polisher in. Still can't believe that there are live sockets in bathrooms in Australia, how dangerous is that?

Now cleaning the carpet, get to the doorway, finish cleaning the carpet take the polisher out and go to unplug the cord. As I walk in the ensuite to pull the plug out, I looked straight in the mirror above the basins, and there sitting with her skirt up and Knicks down, going to the toilet was the owner of the house, the Japanese lady. "Sorry" I said, "but the door was open, and I didn't know you were in there." Still sitting on the toilet, she just said "that's ok". So I unplugged the lead and walked out. Went over to Marinka, and said "you won't believe what just happened." "If it's to do with you I will" she said. "I went to pull the lead out the ensuite, and the lady was sitting on the loo, with her skirt up." "How strange" she said "she has four toilets in the house, and anyway she must have seen you in there, with the lead in the ensuite. She couldn't shut the door any way." "I know, it's odd but I said sorry anyway."

When she came to pay, Marinka said sorry about the toilet incident. "That's ok", was all she said about it. Just as we were going, she asked if she could book us in to clean her lounge suite, and could she have some more fridge magnets for her friends.

Other odd things also happen, like when ladies ask me is it alright to have a shower in their ensuite, while cleaning their bedroom. I say I won't be ten minutes, it's all yours then. But sometimes I am late, and they have a quick shower and then come out in just their towel, and either start talking to me, or go into their walk in wardrobe.

A couple of times women have shown us around the house, opening doors, where their husbands have been naked, getting ready for work, or the kids still in bed. It's worse in the summer because they sleep on top of the bed, with little on. I don't mind the older girls, but the men and boys are just not my thing.

Being Funny

One Friday afternoon a lady rang me, asking if I could clean some lounge suites the next day, being Saturday, she had just moved and her couches had got dirty. I said I could but not until the afternoon, about 1 pm. She lived in Dalkeith, a well known solicitor to the rich and famous. I didn't know at the time but do now. I don't really follow all the celebrity crap. People are people, we all eat, crap, shag and sleep. Some in that order. There are too many wannabees in this world, too much jealousy as well.

That Saturday Marinka came to work with me. We finished our first three jobs by 1 pm and were on our way home, now about 2 pm when I get a phone call from Patti, asking how long will I be. "Just on my way" I said, "we're just running late, sorry I should have called." I completely forgot, wrote the job in the dairy, but forgot to enter it in the computer, so it wasn't on my daily job run.

"Who was that" Marinka asked. "Some solicitor" I said, "forgot all about her, we have to go back to Dalkeith and clean some lounge suites as she has just moved, sorry." "Oh well never mind we're out now, might as well do as much as we can."

So back we went to Dalkeith, from where we were working this morning. One of my favourite suburbs, very old and leafy.

When we got there, there was stuff all over the front porch, looked like a junk yard, mind you everyone's belongings when packed up and piled up looks like junk.

When we went to see the lounge suites, we had to move everything out of the way to get to them. I said jokingly with a straight face, "if I had known you were still in a mess I would have been late." "Well!" She looked at me as if she couldn't believe I just said that, and walked away. I was smiling to myself when I heard Marinka saying to her in the kitchen, "don't take any notice of Peter, he thinks he's funny, but he's not."

Marinka often says I am a lot of things, but funny no. I tend to disagree, I think I am funny at times, it's just that most people don't get my humour, I suppose being brought up, or dragged up in London, you get a sarcastic humour, but I believe if you can't laugh at yourself, than you are too uptight, you can't take life too seriously, that's what I say.

I couldn't been that bad, or I done a really good job, because a week later I went back and cleaned all her leather upholstery, and I can tell you there was masses of it.

Marinka always tells me not to joke with people but sometimes it just comes out like torrents. Now I think I am quite funny, not in a standup comedian way but more of a silly way.

Marinka often accuses me that she is quite often the brunt of my jokes. Well that is not true, only sometimes. The one that still makes me smile is the time we had just moved into a new house, in Halls Head in Mandurah, overlooking the foreshore, and next to the boat ramp, which wasn't so good on weekend mornings for traffic. Quite often we would see a number of dolphins swimming about in the morning, and as my daughter Carly always says, if dolphins can get in so can sharks.

We were only there a short time when I had to go back to England for a few months. While Marinka was there on her own, we had new neighbours, which she got to know.

When I came back a few months later, arriving on the Friday, still jet-lagged, to met the neighbours, I had to go to work on the Monday.

It was a nice sunny morning at about 6 am, as I was leaving the man next door was on his balcony, on the phone have a cup of coffee or tea. "Good morning" I said as I caught his eye, and he nodded.

Marinka walked me to the van in her dressing gown to say goodbye, I gave her a kiss, and said "thanks, I left the money on the side". The neighbour nearly dropped his phone. I just turned around and got in the van, with a grin on my face all the way to my first job.

Marinka was pissed, thinking he thought she was a prostitute, and still today has a go at me about that one, but I can still see the funny side. But as she says you're a lot of things but funny no. Don't know what she means.

Once a girl on the phone while booking in her job, kept changing her mind, and said sorry I am having a blonde moment, and I replied, are you natural blonde or what. She took it as a joke, I think because I had done her job.

On that note of being funny, my favourite one was as follows, but I will have to tell the story from the beginning otherwise you might not think it of it as funny but downright rude or even crude.

To the beginning. I was asked to go around to a house a few years ago when I first started. When I arrived to clean her carpets nobody was at home, so I decided to wait 15 minutes, before I would leave.

After 10 minutes this car puts up as quick as you like up her drive, a girl just in a bikini jumps out and says "sorry I was surfing and forgot the time." Now she was very attractive indeed. "That's ok" I said, just pleased to see her, to do the job I mean.

She said "I will show you the carpets, and then I will get dressed."

"Don't have to on my account" I said, "you look good just the way you are." "Thanks" she said, "then I'll make us a cup of coffee", and she stayed in her bikini I am pleased to say, anything to make the job less boring.

Over the next few years I have worked for her on a number of occasions, and we have always chatted a lot. She told me about being a girl in the fire brigade, about her boy friend, and when she was getting married.

On one occasion, she was having a lot of work done, carpets as well as upholstery, so I took Jason with me, he went to it first, as I was taking bookings on the phone. When I finished I found them both upstairs discussing the job, when I said and to this day don't know why, "hi Lisa you met Jason then", and said to Jason with a straight face, "she's a dirty cow. She likes sliding up and down poles." He for the first time was speechless, and just looked at me in astonishment. I said "it's ok she's a fire woman." "Oh" he said, and grinned. She just laughed.

Still work for her, so it couldn't have been that bad.

Every time I work around the fire women's house I always come back and talk about her, as I probably said before she looks like a young Demi Moore. Marinka and my daughter Carly always just raise their eyebrows, like here we go again, as they both say they know all my stories off by heart now, but I still tell them anyway.

That's part of the fun, if you were to win a race, you want to tell everybody, otherwise it's not as good.

You need to have fun at work, as well as being professional. I believe you can do both. We often joke about cleaning girls rugs, and offer the first one free. My van's licence plate is RUGMEN.

Embarrassing and Sad Stories

I have had two insurance scams done to me that I know of. The first one was quite odd, I should have known better, and followed my gut feeling; normally it doesn't let me down.

I received a call from this lady on my mobile to suggest that I had worked for her before or been recommended by a friend I had worked for. She seemed nice enough on the phone but asked too many questions. She asked if we cleaned white linen lounge chairs and how much for one chair that had bird droppings on, explaining that the bird had flown in to the lounge and landed on her $2,000 arm chair and pooed on the front or the back of the chair.

I explained that there is acid from the birds stomach and that could leave a mark, and the sooner she has it cleaned the better to stop the acids eating into the material. She then booked us in but not for 3 days explaining she had to work.

Now came the interesting part. She asked me would I make it worse? "How could I", I said "you have bird shit on your chair". Then she asked if we were covered by insurance if anything was to go wrong. "Of course we have public liability insurance, just in case, but to date we have never used it" I said and jokingly added "there is always a first time, but we have been doing this for several years now, and we are extremely careful."

"I hope so" she said and put the phone down. Now I knew I should have rung her back and cancelled the job, and told her to get the chair recovered. For two reasons, the first I felt uncomfortable about the phone conversation and second if it was anybody else they would have wanted it done the same day or as soon as possible, more so being such a dear chair. I thought about it, then decided maybe I was being paranoid, and anyway I was going to prove her wrong.

I couldn't do the job but Jason did. Now let me tell you about Jason. He has worked for me for about four years and worked for other carpet cleaners before me, all together has about 10 years experience in the profession of cleaning carpets and upholstery, passed exams, don't know how, and he would be the first to admit he is not the sharpest tool in the box, but good at his job. He actually taught me the first 4 months, straight as you come, in the non sexual sense, honest to a fault.

Jason explained to her the exactly the same as I did, cleaned her chair, got paid and left.

Two days later I had a call from her stating that the chair stain was worse. I agreed to go back and have a look at it, in fact both Jason and myself went together as we were working together that day.

She a had a nice modern house in Cottesloe, stone floors in walkways, timber floors in living areas, good quality furnishings, not that I was that impressed, had seen a lot better, but she seemed to think differently.

She showed us the chair. There was a light brown mark about the size of a one dollar coin. "That looks better than it did" said Jason. I couldn't argue as it was the first time I had seen it. "Not good enough" she said "you told me you could remove it and in fact it's worse." Again I couldn't argue but knew where this was going, thinking back to the phone call. "So you would like to claim on our insurance then for it to be recovered?" I said. "Yes I do, and also there are some water marks on our stone tiles, where Jason sprayed I think he called it brown out on the back of the chair."

How the hell did she remember that? "There might well be water marks as you say, but brown has no PH value so it couldn't be Jason, and if there are water marks like you say, then you had better tell the tiler who laid your floor as he never sealed them correctly."

"Well I tell what we are about to do now is take some photos of your chair, reclean it and I will come in a couple of days and take some more photos along with the photos Jason took before he started and send them to our insurance broker for them to decide."

"I didn't know you took photos of the chair before you cleaned it the first time" she said. "We always take photos when we are not sure of the customer" Jason said, "just to protect ourselves as there are people out there who are not shall I say completely honest."

Emails went back and forward to our insurers, and the lady with the chair after two weeks asked me how things were going, I forwarded the last email I had received from the insurance company not realizing that the first email I sent them stating the facts of the claim, and saying I believe she set out to get her chair recovered by our insurance from the beginning, was attached to it.

Well the next day her husband emailed me stating he was going to take me to court for slander of his wife's name, and they wanted a letter of apology. I replied "I'm sorry you feel like that but we had to fill out a report, and I believe I was correct in my assumptions in the correspondence with your wife." Never heard a thing again from them on the insurance claim, never knew if they were paid. I hope not, but karma ha.

The second time was more subtle. We cleaned the carpets in a house in Wembley Downs and had to dual clean the bedrooms upstairs, and sanitize them because they were so bad.

Anyway they paid us and didn't think any more about the job till about 3 months later when this insurance company calls me and asked me had I worked at that address? Of course I said "yes, why do you ask?" "Well" they said "could you fax us a copy of the original invoice, so we can compare with the invoice they have sent us?" So I did. They called back to thank me and explained the difference, first the new price was $849 and not $349 also they had added the words under my job comments, "due to water damage in the March storms 2010".

Again never heard what the final outcome was, but as you can guess have never worked for either of them again.

After that hail storm in March 2010, we had many calls saying they had water damage due to the storm, most were genuine but some I was not sure, and I suppose so were the insurance companies, it was obvious the real ones, and obvious the scams, but there were a lot in the middle we just didn't know. A lot of people got new carpets in their house that year I know that.

As you are aware when cleaning carpets, you need to move the lounge suites and beds to clean underneath, now you would be surprised what we find, apart from dust, lolly papers, pencils, etc. You would think if somebody was going to move your lounge suite, or bed and more to the point clean your chairs or bed you would check that there was nothing untoward lurking about, and maybe they do, but this chapter is about those that don't.

The most shocking was when Marinka and Jason went to clean some carpets in this quite dirty house. Because of the state of the carpets, Jason asked if they wanted their carpets sanitized. They declined, and said they didn't think they were that bad.

Well when Marinka moved the lounge suite to vacuum underneath she found about twelve carcasses of dead mice in different stages of decay. I couldn't believe it when Jason took some photos of them and sent them to me. They made the owners clean up the mess and we had to sanitize the room before they carried on.

As you can imagine we find many things when cleaning carpets and upholstery, some things I wish we hadn't found, for a few reasons, the first being quite disgusting, the second embarrassing, now you are probably thinking why embarrassing and I will enlighten you.

A lady called me up to clean her carpets as she had been shopping with some friends in Melbourne for the long weekend, and her husband was left on his own, when she came back the house was filthy. He looked like he had had one long party with his mates, and didn't clean up properly and had now gone away to work, so she had decided to get all the carpets cleaned and pay with his credit card.

So around I went. She seemed a nice enough lady, had a quick chat about shopping in Melbourne, and lazy men, and then proceeded to clean her carpets.

In her bedroom I moved her bed to vacuum underneath it, when I found her earrings between the bed and bedside cabinet. Put them in my pocket and carried on cleaning the rest of the house. When I finished, I sat down at the dining room table with her to write out the invoice, she paid me and I was just about to leave, when I remembered the earrings. "By the way I found a pair of your earrings by the side of your bed" I said. "Oh great" she said. Put my hand in my pocket and gave them to her, as she looked at the earrings her face changed, and said "they are not mine." "Oh sorry" I said not knowing what else to say at that moment in time, and then said "maybe they are a present or something." Now quite angry she said "I don't think so do you, you don't know him." I felt like saying "nor do you", but just got up and said "I'd best move on, thanks", said good-bye and walked out never knowing the outcome.

That was probably my worst moment in returning found items. The best was when I found a lady's eternity ring between the carpet and wardrobe. She had lost it for two years, taking it off in her ensuite when washing her hands. It fell off the bench top and rolled away, and she said she searched for hours and never found it. She just gave me a hug and said her husband would be so pleased as he brought it for their tenth wedding anniversary.

She was so chuffed, until a couple of years later, I was around at their new house clearing their tile and grout, and having a coffee in the garden with her husband, and I mentioned the incident with the ring, and said "oh yes I remember that, and she lost it again just before we moved last year." "Well that was a waste of time" I said. "Maybe you could go back and clean the carpets in the old house again for the new people" he said. "I will let you know if I do, she probably will lose it again anyway." "Yeh you're quite right, at least I now have an excuse not to buy her jewellery as she loses it." Good one! Save some money.

One would think if somebody was coming around to clean your carpets, upholstery, or mattress etc you would at least clean up the worst of the stuff from them.

Most do, but lots don't, they leave clothes, including dirty underwear on the floor or mattresses, leave toys, lollies, wrapped and unwrapped, papers, pens, socks etc under the cushions of lounge suites. Some are just covered in dog or cat hair, which I find quite disgusting.

I once found a used Condom under one cushion, and when confronting the owner, she told me it wasn't hers but her daughters. "Well I am still not picking it up" I said. Dirty bitch!

I have found enough money over the years to open a small bank, mostly change. On one occasion I found $50, that was a cheap clean for them.

The most unpleasant jobs are the emergency call outs due to dogs, cats, children, and some adults either being sick or pooing themselves. Apart from the obvious smell, it's the cleaning of all the equipment afterwards, and they must be really clean otherwise we would take it to the next job. The health and safety side is ok because we carry all the right protection, but it still doesn't make the job any better.

Sometimes I feel like a guidance counsellor, for not really knowing people very well and in some cases, meeting them for the first time, they tell you quite personal details of their lives and ask me things as well.

I suppose because I take my own bookings, that they get to know you before I even arrive to do the job. I quite often have a chat over the phone when they are booking in their job. Sometimes I can be quite cheeky, so my wife tells me, but it's more to do with breaking the ice, so they are relaxed when I arrive at their house and don't feel intimidated about me being in their private space.

Four or more years ago (days seem to go quick nowadays) I had a job in City Beach, just had to clean a couple of carpets. When I arrived at the job the front door was about 30 meters up from the drive. Walking up the old brick steps, thinking what the hell am I doing here, I had to take up the equipment yet. I was hoping she wasn't in.

Franchise Of The Year!

She opened the front door before I reached the top, shit I thought. "It's a steep drive isn't it" she said, "you should do it every day with twin girls and shopping." "I would move" I said. "Come in" she said, "I will make us a cup of coffee." Looking up I thought.

She was an English girl, who came from the same part of the country as me, so we chatted quite easily for about 20 minutes, when I said I must get on. They say I can talk for England but she was worse than me.

She had lived there for 2 years with her Australian husband who she met at a friend's party, had twin 3 month old babies, and her mum was coming over to visit next week for the first time. She had only been in Australia for two and a half years, quick marriage, I thought, but hey, I could judge.

She wanted the house clean before her mum arrived, so I was there to clean her bedrooms downstairs, if you can call it downstairs after walking up about 30 just to get to the house.

Once I cleaned the carpets, she made another coffee. I wrote up the invoice and gave her a voucher on other services we do. Had another chat and learned that her husband had brought the house 15 years ago and it needed lots of work doing to it.

He also bought a block behind it for $50,000 at the time, you must understand that than the land was quite unbuildable, but now with modern technology it was worth more than a million as it was close to half an acre. Not that I was impressed, but interested to think how money always goes to money.

She also told me he was a businessman in the city, and had a flat in East Perth where he stayed during the week and came home at weekends. Why people tell me all these things I don't know, maybe they think I would be impressed, or what I don't know, but they do.

She paid me by credit card, his not hers, she didn't have one of her own, strange I thought, but hey, we all live our lives differently. Said goodbye and left with aching legs, bloody stairs.

74

Later that day, she called me on my mobile. I always leave my direct number, just in case clients need to change their bookings or need further work.

After reading through my voucher, she asked if I could come back and clean her bedroom on the top floor, all her drapes and white leather lounge suite. "Of course" I said and booked it in two days before her mum arrived.

Every six months or so after that, I would go around there and clean her carpets, rugs and once her slate floor, hated the job because of the steps, but she was a nice lady.

On the last couple of visits, I noticed she had a black eye, she said she fell down the stairs, on my last visit she had broken her arm, again she said she fell down her steps. I must admit that her stairs where steep, but for obvious reasons I thought her husband was beating her up.

On that last visit and the last time I saw her, she told me she and her husband were not getting on, he had a girlfriend, she was seeing a doctor for depression, and was finding it hard to cope.

I felt really sorry for her but could do nothing, asked why she didn't go back to England if she was so unhappy, but she said she had the twins, and anyway she would go back to nothing.

I asked about friends to help her, she said she didn't have any, but said her mum was coming to visit her soon, and that should help.

When I got home that night I told my wife about her, telling her how bad and depressed she looked. This might be crazy, but you get to know some of your customers really well, they are not like family, but as friends.

A few months passed and she called me up again, saying she and her husband had split up, she was moving out, he had custody of the twins, she was on antidepressants and didn't know what to do. I tried to talk to her but she sounded like she was drinking. That night when I got home I told Marinka all about the conversation, she called her and asked if she wanted to come over to our place for a few days, or at least come over for dinner, to get away from it all and have a chat and a rest. She said she would think about it.

Never heard no more from her until she called a few weeks later, and told me she had moved to a rental down the road still in City Beach. I booked her job in, but had to send the boys there as I was too busy at the time. They said she seemed ok, but a little down, she had her twin girls with her.

Then about 6 months later she called, on a Monday to get her carpets cleaned on the Wednesday as she had a rent inspection that week. I couldn't do Wednesday, but booked her in on the Thursday, decided that I would definitely clean them myself this time to see how she was doing. When I got around there a car was on the drive, but no one was at home, knocked a few times, then rung her mobile, again no answer, looked around the house thinking she might be in the garden, no sign of life. Tried knocking again, rung her mobile again, still no answer, left my card, got in the van and left, feeling rather strange.

Tried call her over the next two days, but just got her answering machine, she never called back.

Thought about her over the last year, but never heard or saw from her again and often wondered how she and her girls where, until a couple of weeks ago, I worked for her neighbour, two doors away from her old house.

"Did you know your old neighbour with the two twin girls, who live two doors down", I asked. "I haven't seen her since she moved", I said, "about a year ago I went around to her new house to clean her carpets but she wasn't there, left messages, but never heard from her again which was strange."

"You don't know do you," she said, "a year ago she committed suicide." "Oh shit, I knew she was depressed, and at one time tried to help her, but didn't know she was that bad, how sad, what happened to the girls?" "Their father's first wife has custody of them." "How strange" I said. "Yes I know, I didn't know her that well, but knew their marriage was volatile, I tried to help a few times myself, but she always said she was ok."

"Sad though, any way this might be the last time you come here." "Why's that" I said. "We are separating." "Oh I am sorry." "That's life" she said. I've known them for at least 5 years also.

Doesn't matter how long you live, life still surprises you, every so often.

I've listened to so many stories over the years, it's impossible to remember them all, but the really sad or funny one stick in your mind.

Another sad story started with a phone call from her sister. She asked me to clean her lounge suite, and a couple of rugs, around her house. While I was there, she asked if I could do some work around her younger sister's house, a few streets away. I couldn't that day, but arranged to go around the next day. She said she wanted to pay for it, because her sister was feeling a bit tender at the moment. "Ok" I said, "I will do her job but invoice you." Got her address and details, noted her phone number, by all accounts her sister had lost her phone.

The next day when I arrived at her sisters, the thing I noticed was they didn't look alike, this one was a lot thinner, and looked older, not younger than her.

"Hi" I said, "show me what you want done and I will make a start." "Did my sister tell you she was paying for it" she asked. "Yes" I said, "she said you where feeling a bit tender, so she said she wanted to pay for the job, I am going to invoice her once I am done."

"Bit tender is a good description for how I am" she said, and with that lifted up her top. She had a scar from between her boobs going all the way down to her knickers line, and maybe beyond.

She than showed me the other scars on her arms, legs and back. She looked like Frankenstein in a horror movie.

Franchise Of The Year!

She then went on to tell me her ex had come around unexpectedly two days before Christmas, that was four months ago, she had kicked him out two months before that, because he had became a druggy, and got in with the wrong people. He forced his way in demanding to share their two kids aged 4 and 6 years old. Luckily the kids were at her mums for the evening; he then punched her 30 times, and then got the kitchen knife and stabbed and slashed the over 45 times. She passed out and doesn't remember any more until she woke up in Hospital, by all accounts the neighbours called the police and her sister, because of all the noise.

Her sister got there first and found her in a pool of blood, thought she was dead, but the paramedics arrived shortly afterwards and saved her life, obviously not her time. I got the later part of that story from her sister when she paid the bill. He had been arrested awaiting a trial. Can't say any more for obvious reasons.

In 2008 there was a fire in Wembley Downs Shopping Centre, caused by an electrical fault in the roof space, and the entire shopping centre burnt down. Many of the local residents watched the display, as it was on a Saturday morning, even the emergency services advised them not to, due to the toxic chemicals in the air, but what else have some people got to do on a Saturday?

A couple of weeks later I was working around one of our regular customer's house. She was a lovely lady, about 60 years old, a teacher at a local school, never married, still dresses like she did in the hippy sixties, spends all her spare time travelling the world, normally the most unusual and remote destinations. We were talking about the fire, when she said that she also watched the shopping centre burn. She lives a few streets away, but could smell it, so she went for a sticky beak, but not till later that afternoon.

While she was waiting there, she was standing close to an ambulance on the over side of the road, on a vacant block. She was saying that she thought that some people must have been caught inside the centre while it was burning, because she could smell burning flesh.

So went up to the fire-fighter who was on a break, and asked him if there were any people inside when it caught fire. "No" he said, "what makes you think that?"

"Well I thought I could smell burning flesh", she said. With a smile he said "I think you will find that smell is the sausages cooking on the bar-b-cue that someone is cooking for our dinner, while we are here." Going bright red, she said "of course", and walked quickly home.

Conclusion

The week before Christmas, our busiest week of the year, we had three vans on the road.

I was driving home on the Wednesday evening, come down the Freeway, when I heard a large bang. The vans engine died, but fortunately I was in the inside lane. I coasted to the emergency lane, lifted the bonnet, where steam was pouring out. Waited a while for it to cool down, unlocked the radiator cap and filled it with clean water we keep in the van.

Waited another twenty minutes, then tried to start the engine, no luck, so I called my mechanic Paul, who's great, but he was too far away, but said if I could tow it home he would come around later and have a look. I called Marinka, who came down and picked me up. We decided to leave the van there and tow it back ourselves later when it was quieter on the roads. I have towed cars many a time when I was young, she had never done it.

That night at eight o'clock we set out. Got to the van, roads pretty quiet, tied the tow rope on, and said to Marinka "do you want to tow or be towed?"

"What's easier?" she asked. "Neither" I said, "if you tow you have to be careful you pull away really slowly, no jerking, allow enough time for traffic, be careful at lights. If you are being towed you have to make sure the rope is always tight, watch for my brake lights, don't keep your foot on the brake, otherwise it's impossible to tow." "Being towed seems easier", she said. 'Are you sure?" "Yes."

I got into the Triton and she got into the Mercedes Vito and away we went, slow as I could, as she had never done this before. I could feel she was putting the brakes on quite a bit as we were travelling. We had to go about ten kms but it seemed a lot longer. We turned off the Freeway as soon as possible, and went down Marion Avenue, but there was of course lots of traffic lights and roundabouts, so lots of stops and starts. By now it was also getting dark and harder to see. By the time we got home, Marinka was as white as a sheet, and shaking,

Her hands hurt as she was gripping the steering wheel so tight. Shouting in anger, she said "why didn't you tell me it was that hard to be towed?" "I did" I said, "you could have been the tow-er." "I am never going to that again in my life it's too scary." "Sorry" I said, "I thought you might have realized how hard it is."

One of the boys picked me up in the one of the other two vans the next morning. I had spent the night before moving jobs around, so we could do three runs with two vans, and I thought it should work out ok, even if we had to work late. Paul the mechanic was going to look at the broken van that day. Four days before I was going on holiday, couldn't wait for the rest.

We had just gone about ten kilometres down the road, when the clutch on the van just hit the floor while we were in a traffic queue. We limped to a lay-by. I rung Paul who said he would look at the van, when he came up to check the other van, but looks like the hydraulic clutch had gone in the Mercedes Vito, not a cheap job. "Fuck" I said, "I can't believe my luck. I had just changed all the jobs now I have to do it again."

I called Marinka and told her, between us we agreed if we could limp through this day we would hire a trailer for tomorrow, and work from that if we couldn't get one of the vans back on the road. We loaded the upholstery equipment only in her Toyota Yaris, that was the smallest of all the equipment. We did the upholstery, while the other boys did the other jobs in the only van left. The first was fucked and would need a new engine plus other bits, costing in excess of $7,000, the van was not worth that so I sold it for $1,000 for parts, it had a gas conversion kit in it. The other van wouldn't be ready till after Christmas.

So we had to hire a trailer for four days until we broke up for Christmas. We survived but only just.

We had a good holiday in Kuala Lumpur.

Just came back to a large bill for the new clutch.

We have over the years, as you have read, had good times, bad times, some happy, some sad, and heard and seen some funny stories.

Just when things are going well, life has a way of bring you back to earth, like there is an equilibrium. All things must equal out. If you earn money, you seem to pay out more. Just when you think you have worked it all out, something happens to doubt yourself, and start again.

We have tried to build the business against the odds, not only for profit but for self pride. Also because many have told us that certain things can't be done, when we believe that they could, or at least we gave them a go. Have always tried to do the right thing, even when it has cost us money.

Tried different things and tried to think outside the square, by doing freebees to get commercial work (e.g. cleaning reception areas).

As they say you can please some of the people some of the time, but not all the people all the time, or a better version, you can't please all the people all the time, so just please yourself.

As we say when we have a toast, here's to those who wish as well, those who don't, can go to hell.

I still enjoy my job, and when I don't that's the time to call it a day, and sell the business.

That day will come I have no doubt, but hopefully I could be involved in a similar business. I would never buy another franchise, I know that, with what I have learnt from the one I am with, and listened to our different franchisees from other companies, they are all much the same.

It would not be that hard now to start one's own business from scratch, do the research, marketing and advertising.

If I was to franchise anything, I would do the following things:

1. Cut down on office staff, far too many Chiefs doing the same job.

2. Let each indivisible franchisee do their own advertising, or as a State group together and advertise. Saving each franchisee $41,600 they pay to the Franchise each year, and using that money to suit their needs not the company as a whole.

3. Send the chemicals in concentrated form, saving on containers and freight.

4. Put the call centre in Australia, or Australians in the Philippines.

5. Each State to have a business development program.

6. Each State to have 6 monthly meetings on advertising etc.

7. Listen more to franchisees instead of thinking they are not as bright as you.

8. Have incentive packages i.e. monthly awards. Best upselling or new customers, or conversion rate.

9. Personal call to each franchisee every month to see how they are going and can head office help in any way.

10. Answer e-mails.

I think I would not only miss my regular customers I have known for years, but also the thrill of getting new ones, and meeting people for the first time, hearing new stories and sharing some of mine with them.

May be the next five years will be easier, with just as many funny times and stories.